Benchmarks

Other Books in the Alaska Literary Series

The Cormorant Hunter's Wife, by Joan Kane (poetry)

The Rabbits Could Sing, by Amber Thomas (poetry)

The City Beneath the Snow, by Marjorie Kowalski Cole (fiction)

Oil and Water, by Mei Mei Evans (fiction)

Upriver, by Carolyn Kremers (poetry)

Gaining Daylight, by Sara Loewen

Benchmarks

New and Selected Poems
1963-2013

by Richard Dauenhauer

University of Alaska Press
Fairbanks

University of Alaska Press
P.O. Box 756240
Fairbanks, AK 99775-6240

Library of Congress Cataloging-in-Publication Data
Dauenhauer, Richard.
[Poems. Selections]
Benchmarks : new and selected poems 1963–2013 / by Richard Dauenhauer.
       pages cm
ISBN 978-1-60223-209-9 (paperback : acid-free paper) — ISBN 978-1-60223-210-5
(electronic)
I. Title.
PS3554.A84B46 2013
811ʾ.54—dc23
                              2012048322

Cover design by Kristina Kachele
Cover illustration © Jim Marks

This publication was printed on acid-free paper that meets the minimum
requirements for ANSI / NISO Z39.48–1992 (R2002) (Permanence of Paper for
Printed Library Materials).

for Nora

Nel mezzo del cammin di nostra vita. . . .
In the middle of the journey of our life. . . .
—Dante, *Divine Comedy*

Home is where one starts from. As we grow older
The world becomes stranger, the pattern more complicated
Of dead and living. Not the intense moment
Isolated, with no before and after,
But a lifetime burning in every moment
And not the lifetime of one man only
But of old stones that cannot be deciphered.
　　　　　　　　　　—T. S. Eliot, "East Coker V"

Death is not the end of life, but the beginning of its renewal.
　　　　　　　　　—Bishop Kallistos (Ware)

Precious in the sight of the Lord is the death of his saints.
　　　　　　　　　—Psalm 116:15

The honey of peace in old poems.
　　　　　　　　　—Robinson Jeffers,
　　　　　　　　　"To the Stone Cutters"

Contents

Acknowledgments

I thank the following journals, anthologies, and broadside publishers in whose pages these new poems first appeared, sometimes in earlier versions: *Alaska Native Reader, Alaska Quarterly Review, ASLA* (Helsinki), *Café Solo, Hyperion, Ice Floe, Inroads, Northern Review,* Peter Jon Gillquist, *Quixote, Sky's Own Light, Syracuse 10,* and *Tidal Echoes.*

Selected poems were chosen from the following previously published books and chapbook. I am grateful to these publishers and their editors for their faith in and support of my work, and I include the editors' names in parentheses.

Glacier Bay Concerto, © 1980 by Alaska Pacific University Press, published by Alaska Pacific University Press, 1980 (O. W. Frost).

The Shroud of Shaawát Séek', © 1983 by Richard Dauenhauer, published by Orca Press, 1983 (Cheryl Morse).

Frames of Reference, © 1987 by The Black Current Press, published by The Black Current Press, 1987 (Ron and Suzanne Scollon).

Phenologies, © 1986 by Richard Dauenhauer, published by Thorp Springs Press, 1988 (Paul Foreman).

I also thank again the editors of journals in which some of the poems from my above-listed earlier books first appeared:

In *Phenologies: Afterthought, Beloit Poetry Journal, Harpoon, Hyperion.*
In *Glacier Bay Concerto: Poets and Players.*
In *Frames of Reference: Alaska Journal, Axios, Beloit Poetry Journal, Crab Creek Review, Dog River Review, Gold Dust, Greenfield Review, Harpoon, Heartland, In the Dreamlight, Loonlark/Orca Anthology 1983, Northward Journal, Salvage, Syracuse 10.*

Thanks to Suzanne and Rachel Scollon for their comments on the earliest draft of the manuscript. I thank the editors, board, and readers of the University of Alaska Press for their encouragement and advice, especially Peggy Shumaker, Sheila Nickerson, Emily Wall, and John Morgan for their close reading of the evolving manuscript and their suggestions for improvement. Thanks also to Kathy Ruddy for her proofreading of the final draft, and to Sue Mitchell and Natalie Taylor for their very careful copyediting.

New Poems, Part One:

The Genealogy of Beer

In Praise of the Neolithic

Restoring the creek bed
and drainage past the house,
when suddenly a rock
slices through my work glove
and through my fingertip.
I cleanse the wound by sucking,
rinse my finger in a mouth
of Scotch, unblended but
for blood, and staunch the flow
by wrapping tight and holding
my sweat-stained handkerchief;
apply a band-aid when the blood
flow stops, continue working
in gentle rain, respectful
of stones that have been there
since the forming of the earth.

The Genealogy of Beer
(A Blend of Beck's and Guinness Stout)

—in Memory of Timothy Donoghue (1815–1894)
and Jane Kingston Donoghue (1819–1865)

The Irish plumbers spot my empty case
of Guinness Stout, and ask me where I ever
learned to drink it. I trace my bloodlines
on my mother's side: the Burkes and Cavanaughs
from Galway; my mother's father's mother's line
the farthest back we go is Timothy
Donoghue, from Ireland, who moved
in 1839 to Merrickville,
Ontario—Timothy Donoghue
from Bandon, County Cork, who had studied
to be a priest. Before he was ordained
became an Anglican (how fortunate
for us!) and on the boat to Canada
met and fell in love—Jane Kingston, too,
from County Cork. So here we are, through lines
of Newman. The borderline is "Grier,"
my mother's father. English? Irish? Scotch?
It all depends on who you're talking to.
My father's side transparent from the name,
Dauenhauer, Dauben-hewer, stave
maker, only found in German wine-
producing lands. We're back to -hugh,
with Dono-ghue and Dauen-hugh. My name's
a barrel of a medieval name
emptied of its former meaning, old
names and countries always being drained—
the working draft of North America,
filled with spirits from around the world.

Loving in the Autumn Rain

Rain above,
    the waterbed below,

all this liquid
    returning to the earth—

the sounds of rain
    falling on the roof tin

funneling in drainpipes,
    overflowing cistern,

waterfall and small stream
    swelling to the sea:

superfluous,
    this gift of fluids

far beyond what's needed
    for returns,

the sacrament of love
    remains,

after enough
    all the more.

Homeric Erotica

Hexameters
of lingerie and leather:

we really need
another word in English,
euzoneous, to capture
the intentions of the Greek,
meaning *softly belted*,
further defined as
"unrestricted usage;
always of or pertaining to
a non-Greek female
prisoner of war."

When I was a teen, a Trojan
was something else again.
But now with AIDS
in epic proportion
it's okay to show them.
More difficult to talk
of Hector's helmet,
and what choice has Briseis
when Agamamnon wants her
and Akhilleus' pride
is hurt
while every night some slave girl
serves in some Akhaian's bed.

In bronze age economics
a winner gets a tripod
worth twelve oxen; the loser—
a woman worth but four.
At funeral games,
the prizes: cauldrons, tripods,
mules and horses, oxen,
and softly belted girls; a girl
adept at gentle handicraft
to be taken by the winner
who took the prizes
and handed the woman
over to his men.

All this for Helen
who can't decide
whose bed to spread her thighs in.

Anna

(Feast of the Dormition of Saint Anne,
July 25/August 8)

Icon strokes
of Joachim and Anna
as they snuggle
by the temple doors:

flashbacks
of the marriage bed,
verifying cosmic
archetypes of love:

"Woman, lovely
in her bones," as
wife, as grand-
mother of God.

Anniversary Poem (1988)

—for Nora

Near fifty, to see the naked women
well in centerfolds, one removes his glasses,
peers, nose close. Bifocals no longer do.

The sweet young things grow farther out of sight,
immortalized in all the magazines
that I no longer buy, nor can afford to.

How better now the long familiar touch
of nakedness: in darkness, varied parts
of bodies deep at night, in touch with one

another, needing now no reference point
than love, when love is truly blind.

Lunchtime at Taguchi's
(An idyll for Sam and the Gang)

—*In memory of Juneau's finest greasy spoon restaurant and in memory of Sam Taguchi, January 22, 1918–December 20, 1995, and Takeshi "Gim" Taguchi, March 27, 1924–June 9, 1997*

South Franklin Street, where paint's
been peeling for a hundred years:
Taguchi's Tea House, "Fine
Chow"—corned beef, adobo,
steamed black cod, pork noodles,
Britain burger deluxe—
cholesterol galore,
nerve center of the world,
where fishermen and new
natives in three-piece suits
navigate each noon
through fog-bank grease. On walls,
like channel markers, photo-
graphs, a gallery
of local heroes: Sam
Samaniego glances
from his boat, and Michael
Avoian ("Bingo") beams
proudly by his lamp,
and Tiger Olson from Taku
turns briefly from his beer;
the empty stool, where Vern
Metcalfe held his court all
afternoon. And others,
also mostly gone now,
chart shores of memory
past which the living move
to crowd at counterspace

or share a table, to
sustain ourselves above
our humble bowls below
these men immortalized
like figures on a Grecian urn.
This could be anywhere,
yet nowhere else but here.
We linger over food,
through steamy windows view
the people passing,
forever beautiful.

Chemawa School Cemetery
(Founded 1886)

In my arms I carry Jon, age one,
part Tlingit, as we search the grass for grave
markers of departed Tlingit students,
relatives or in-laws, when we find
the 1918 graves of Aleuts
whose names survive: Merculieff, Ermanoff,
Rukovishnikoff. I softly sing them
"Memory Eternal" in Slavonic.

A sunny day in spring, the last of April,
a muggy afternoon of nettles, bees.

Amtrak clacks the rails that separate
the cemetery from the old, brick school
building, now abandoned, passing through
to Portland; sounds its horn. Again I heft
the baby, changing arms, keeping up the search
for Tlingit names like Zuboff, Dick, and Jackson,
my shoe tip clearing, polishing the name-plates
on graves of those who never made it home.

August Afternoon at
Helle's Pool, Vancouver, Washington

—for Bob and Pat

We float the pool, the buzz
of locusts or cicadas, hiss
of phony plastic inner tubes
leaking underneath us. We lament
the rarity, the near extinction
of childhood inner tubes,
by definition: too used
and patched to put back on
cars or trucks or tractors.
We change positions, heads
and armpits through the tubes now,
like some mythic heroes being
born through clamshells from the warm
womb of the void. Our wives,
more cynical, from poolside
describe the myth as giant
geoduck and garlic.

Jamie, Racing Off

Granddaughter Jamie, now
fourteen, downhill racer
in braces, embracing

speed, off to Statewide
and next the Western
Regionals, all aglow.

Yesterday in France
in the Winter Olympics
her older teammate

Hilary Lindh took home
a silver medal
in the women's downhill

and Juneau goes crazy
with welcome home posters.
I superimpose

our flashbacks of Jamie—
color slides and prints: first
downhill on the bunny

slope in gold and silver
winter sunlight; first
ski-steps, cross-country

with Grandma; very first
steps across our living-
room, the rug once stained

with brown-spot, diaper leak.
But now, with Jamie three
weeks shy of fifteen, now

in love with speeds that none
of us has ever reached—
it's me scared crapless.

Soccer Squad

—for our granddaughters: Andi, Rissa, Jamie, Teresa

Like storm winds
off the glacier
that looms above the soccer field:

the Ransom and Florendo girls
charge downfield,
eyes and cleats

gleaming in the sun.
How wonderful for them
to be teenage girls;

how wonderful for me
not to be
a teenage boy or goalie.

Red Dogs and Onions

—for Tag Eckles (a.k.a. Professor Phineas Poon, whom I preferred to call
Euphonious, May 24, 1950–July 26, 2009), for John Wilson,
and for the Juneau Fencing Club in general

I think of Liberace
playing to casino
crowds to make a living:

and our local cronies,
competent musicians all,
inspired composers

donning summer garters,
masks of gold rush drama,
playing on the sawdust floors

as general practitioners
of song, dosing out scandal
as much as they can take,

or as their needs require,
to waves of aging tourists
deposited to ply

Alaska streets by shiploads,
where sleaze becomes nostalgia
for a reinvented past.

Tumor (1996)

Stricken. Close to death how many times,
accumulating symptoms. X-rays show
the tumor now, at last, and we expect
the other shoe to drop, but can't know when
or how, uncertainty intensified
by all the things we do together now.

We walk the beach in August sunlight, hand
in hand, the days of radiance and trans-
figuration, sometimes separate,
exploring on our own, but never far
away. We watch the salmon stream at low
tide, the living images of dying
generations, and we think, but never
quite articulate our fear: will each
sacrament of love or summer day
in sun together somehow be our last?

Croquet, Nickerson Pitch

—*for Martin Nickerson, home team coach,*
and for Sheila Nickerson

It looks so civil, simple, innocent.
And then you learn—it's all in strategy,
and nice guys finish last. We resurrect
this seeming silliest of games. It all
comes back to me from childhood farther south,
as here, approaching summer solstice far
north of those Long Island courts, our coach
recalls his styles from childhood—grips and swings
of grandmothers and maiden aunts, and each
little old lady with the meanest mallet
in the east. On this rarity tonight—
a level lawn along Alaska fjords—
we cultivate from former time and place
what seems the gentlest of games—until
veneers are blasted off with each roquet.
Our necks beneath the feet of conquerors,
helpless, moved a mallet head away.
Politely grinning, comes roquet, the stroke
an execution axe. But less-known rules
describe heroic "Rovers"—players who,
having moved through every wicket, now,
electing not to hit the turning post
in triumph, turn to help their team,
returning to the field in sacrifice
like Buddha, entering again the ring
of death and birth on courts around the world.

Breakfast at Grandma Nora's

—for Cole, Gabe, Mikaela, Grandma Nora, and Grandma Le

Cole (age 6) is into
rocks and drawing Zuni
symbols. He demonstrates
on paper, shows his crystal,
and tells about his rock
collection. Grandma Nora
shows her rocks to Cole.
Every fossil, every
pebble has a story:
Alsek River rafting,
Copper River fishing,
jars of Anchorage
volcanic ash. They trade.

Gabe (age 4) is con-
trary today. He spec-
ulates on pancakes:
"I'm gonna feed my butt
and poop out my mouth!"

Grandma Nora expounds
on coprolites, the poop
that turns to stone. What a
concept! Fossil doo-doo!
The final word on turds.

The Facts of Life

Grandma Le and grandsons
    discuss where babies come from.

Says Aiden Phillip
    (going on seven),

"I was an action figure.
    I came out of a Lucky
        Charms box."

Image of Nora, Rendering Seal Oil

Like a priest of pre-
Vatican Two, serving
requiem in black:
vested in a plastic
garbage bag, bending
over sacramental
seal fat, rendering
as oil this gift of life
from younger hunters,
working on the back porch
in deference to seal
grease—incense of its own.

Translating Pasternak

We are His poem.
                        —Ephesians 2:10

The season of Nativity again
and I return to poetry as prayer,
not putting trust in princes, sons of men;
try to escape complacency, determine

to respond to images—how old is new
from Psalms to Ferlinghetti, Pasternak—
the insights, inspiration, here and now.
Respond as they responded to the knock

of wording from eternity in wait
for human life through cooperation
and consent; allow the word to integrate
and nurture, through compassion, meditation.

It's time to give myself a Christmas gift,
my promise to myself to translate Pasternak,
his "Christmas Star" for starters, waiting list
of thirty years accumulated clock

ticking off my last creative life,
never finding time enough for poems.
I learn anew. Each time I come alive,
re-energized from this, expanding time

as poetry breaks through to other worlds.
Translation: like the tail of a comet,
pulled by the gravity of uncommon words
through which I navigate by lexicon

to struggle with and feel his poetry—
jazz-like rhythm, assonance, outrageous rhyme.
His poet—hostage of eternity
and prisoner of time.

Awaiting Discharge

At least when you woke up in the hospital, you knew
you hadn't died and gone to heaven.
                    —Bishop Seraphim (Sigrist), in conversation

It wasn't lost on Chaucer's Wife of Bath,
I tell myself, sitting here, impatient
for home. Reflecting on the aftermath
of surgery, my winter's discontent,

I know my favorite things are trivial—
that I can live without them—but, like Bartleby,
would rather not. After days of hospital
cuisine, I want my own concocted tea,

my own reclining chair, my own TV
remote control, coffee, food. Procedure:
extreme ureterolithotomy—
(dig out a kidney stone). Like my father

I'm on the bed-edge, antsy for return
to more familiar forms. Rhymes come to me
from centuries ago, of "yearn" and "urine."
Life's incomplete without the poetry.

I sit in Dad-like grubby sweats, low-cut
rubber boots; reflect, how even with a youthful nurse
inspecting, there's nothing much erotic
about the study of your catheter.

The Wife of Bath: an early theologian,
organ donor with well-argued discourse
alluding to Saint Paul how the organ
of urination's used for intercourse.

"For business and for pleasure, equipment
given to man and woman both," quoth she,
"I'll use as freely as my maker sent
to serve in marriage, not virginity."
The place of love—a place of excrement.

Based, of course, on hearsay

(Based, of course, on hearsay—
the folk tradition now
illegal), "This is how
we ate them, once a year."

Take only from a nest
with one or two eggs.
If there are three eggs, there's
an embryo inside.

Appreciate the weathered,
speckled-granite look
of the rock-like egg.

Boil gently,
eat when warm.

Crack, peel, cut.
Lightly salt and pepper,
drizzle seal oil
on the orange yolk to taste.

Savor the faintly fishy taste
from seagulls feasting
on the herring run.

Epiphany 2008

Juneau: we grouse about the rain every
Epiphany, looking for a dry place
to bless the water. On rain-slick ice, in snow-
generating slush, we try to bless

the outside waters, water unprotected
by some church roof, by structures we create
to organize creation, so we go
with the flow. This January, Forefeast

in pouring rain, the Feast itself in fog,
wrapping us with images—the mantle
of Elijah passed; the dew of Gideon
here on fleece and earth alike, on boats

and mountainsides, pervasive, having turned
everywhere to binding ice—then gift
of alpenglow on dove-white peaks as daybreak
promises: somewhere south of here, the sun.

Sensory Overload

(Viewing the Buddhist Tapestries at the *Sacred Arts of Bhutan Exhibit*, Honolulu Academy of Arts, April 2008)

Protecting the Dharma, Lady
of Long Life rides her snow lion
on a moon disc above a lotus,
emerging from a pond full
of jewels and water birds.

Compassionate Boddhisatvas,
find it impossible
to help out all humanity
single handedly, whence

the multiplicity of heads
and hands, to see the needs of each,
for lending each of us a hand.
Hyperbole to the max!

Waikiki, the Breakers

Waikiki, the breakers
fifty years too late
for me. I spent my youth
on Adirondack ponds
gunwale pumping Grumman
canoes. We made our own
surf, pumped single footed
on the miniscule back
deck. We were the surf
and breakers, the biggest frogs
in smallest ponds, nothing
like the mid-Pacific
ocean. This would have been
fantastic, but I think
we made a bigger splash.

Sonnet on National Security in the Bush-Cheney Reign
(Lines Disclosed in a Doctor's Waiting Room)

—for Ron and Suzie, my erstwhile editors,
who insisted that my poems be as long as my epigraphs.

Part I
Epigraph as Action

> 9. National Security and Intelligence Activities. We may release health information to authorized federal officials for intelligence, counter-intelligence, and other national security activities as authorized by law.

> 10. Protective Services for the President and Others. We may disclose health information to authorized federal officials so they may provide protection to the President, other authorized persons, or foreign heads of state, or to conduct special investigations.
> —Release form to be signed before receiving medical attention

Part II
Sonnet as Reaction

> How flattering to learn my ailment
> has spread to national security—
> minute attention given to the least
> of us, new forms of medical consent,
>
> assurances that finally our coverage
> is universal. We agree to probes
> for polyps, fistulas, and kidney stones—
> homeland security with rubber gloves

exploring not the body politick,
but us, for pre-existing conditions,
symptoms, and attitudes of commission,
and if their scan's for anything poetic

will, like Mandelstam on Stalin's moustache,
this sonnet make a presidential splash?

After Finishing an Activities Report for the Dean

A dark autumnal afternoon. I walk
my customary path along the lake,
the summer greenery now turning red
and yellow, brown, the lake at best reflecting
gray of sky and low-hanging rain clouds
heading this way. Reflecting on my past,
I think of German poetry, the line
komm in den totgesagten Park und schau,
come in to the park they say is dead and look.

A haunting image, coping with decline,
to look for meaning at the end of life,
to look for understated brilliance still
alive. On certain days, it's difficult
to find. More German poems, Rilke's
"summer was so great," but here and now
there never was a summer; maybe this
is all there is and all there is to be—

a pattern we're reluctant to admit,
dissatisfied, and yet, afraid to let
it go, forever taking on too much,
afraid of missing some. Medieval
poetry now haunts me: *owê war sint
verswunden alliu mîniu jâr,* oh where
have all my years of lifetime disappeared?
*Ist mir mîn leben getroumet, oder
ist ez wâr,* was all my life
dreamed up for me, or is it really true?
Ou sont les neiges d'antan, where are the snows
of yesteryear, curriculum of life?

Dating Myself

—for the University of Alaska Southeast Beatniks

In folklore class today
discussing lovers' lanes
and urban legends,
I used the word
"necking," creating some
discussion. Two co-eds
had never heard the word
before, but were
delighted with the image.
"It worked for me
in high school," I replied.

I should have done some
fieldwork on the spot,
asking what they do
these days on dates,
and what they call it now.

I should have mentioned verbs
like "spooning," told tales
from my grandfather's day
like dropping the buggy
whip, and walking back
to get it, if you had
to pee, but couldn't raise
that subject on a date.

Thoughts after Working on Salmon Eggs from our Grandson

I was never any good at tennis,
always lofting the ball over
the fence. My racquet, forty-five years old
easily, now put to better use
for straining caviar. The Yakutat
technique for *ikura*: brine four to one
for maybe half an hour, then rub egg
sacks over tennis racquet; drain and freeze
in jars or Ziploc bags. Or fresh—enjoy
Russian style with onion, butter, soda
crackers, shots of frozen Stoly, neat.

Forwarding John Updike's "Baseball" on *The Writer's Almanac*, June 22, 2009

—in memory of Andy Hope (December 23, 1949–August 7, 2008)
and Jim Bowen (May 20, 1951–April 25, 2010)

My first reaction was, like scooping up
a grounder, to shoot it to first base,
to forward it to you by email, but,
poised to throw, I realize there's no
one there to catch it. No one else I know
would love this poem more. You died almost
a year ago. I knew that. I know that.
But yet one more reminder catches me
off guard. We hold these things we want to share,
stand looking at them like a baseball glove,
no longer knowing where to throw the ball.

Unfinished Business

Retirement plans: first,
turn potato garden,
plant potatoes; start to
shred old paperwork, old
IRS returns, bank
statements; then fly south for
cancer surgery; spend
the summer getting well,
return to thirty years
of Tlingit texts to finish,
edit poetry,
and watch potatoes grow.

Triptych: Easter 2011

I
From childhood up, we know
the story, witness it
confirmed in lives of friends
and family, and then
ourselves: cancer,
a wake-up call that death,
no longer a distant
concept, is coming soon.

II
We become the lines
of ancient poetry
like Kogutey,
Altai, from Central Asia,
"His past days lengthened,
his coming days grew short."

III
The text: Gesthemene.
Even Jesus didn't
want to die. No one
wants to die. But Christ
accepted. We prepare
to meet the promise of
the empty tomb.

Joyriding

April 27, still too cold
to read outside, even in morning sun.
I go indoors, our southeast corner room,
don my baseball hat against the sun,
and read my mystery. Usually I ride
my exercise bike, but today I bask
in greenhouse warmth, deeply rooted in my
recliner, as the earth slowly takes me
orbiting the vernal morning sun,
and I pretend it's summer and I have
no obligations, nothing else to do
but ride the earth into the working day.

Gardening with Elijah

Gardening with five-
year-old great-grandson
Elijah, preparing
to plant potatoes,
we unearth eternal
questions: the anatomy
of worms, the rising
steam, where sunbeams
meet the fresh-turned earth.

Meditation on Dandelions
in Morning Sunlight

Surely there are still
morning glories there
where I planted them
more than sixty years ago
in the starter garden
of my childhood. Years later
my parents must have spent
endless energy each
season rooting out last
vestiges, forever
encroaching on flowers
of adulthood. Somehow seed
endures beyond design.

New Poems, Part Two: Juneau Sketches

Daanaawaak / Silver Dollar Eye:
Supermarket Satori

I've known this Tlingit name
for over forty years.
The world at large has known it
a century or more
through Muir and other
Alaska travel books:
Daanaawaak, Silver Eye, or,
more precisely, Silver
Dollar Eye. Today I
see it for the first time
here, now, as this enormous
parking lot Raven perched
on my top carrier
looks at me and blinks
like an eye doctor
sliding down another
lens for you to try,
and suddenly, you see.

Phenomenology of Moss

—for Robin Kellerer

So out of shape, so
hiking slowly, so no-
ticing so many
mosses by the trail-
side, naming them
starburst, birdsfoot, pipe-
cleaner, dreadlocks;

others nondescript
beyond generic
carpet, so remain
metaphorless,
each simply being
something in itself.

Shark Fins

Shark fins, circling for
the kill: stones on spring ice, cast
by cautious skaters.

Easter Monday

Easter Monday:
avalanche guns
sound in April
sunlight, final
salvos in the
war with winter.

Song Sparrow

Song sparrow, badged in treetop
April-morning spotlight,
framed in alder buds
auditioning new song.

Ear-shattering

So ear-shattering:
the sound of hummingbird wings,
summer, 4 AM.

July 5, 2009

Dawn: Song sparrow, air
gunpowder-thick from midnight
fireworks.

Sunrise

Kayak at slack tide
slices dawn-flat sea, flashes
dripping paddle blades.

Daybreak

Daybreak: steady
rainfall. White spurts
of junco tails erupt
like lightning bolts, like
scissors cutting up-
ward, earth to lowest
spruce and hemlock, slice
undifferentiated dawn.

Through Study Window

Across the highway,
in summer morning
sunbeams,
articulating dew—

a thrush moving
on a stump:

with further study,
reveals itself
like an Athabaskan
riddle,

as, tentative,
a twitching ear,
the only motion
of a doe.

Iambics for the Southeast Alaska Regional Cross-Country Meet September 20, 2003

The smell of analgesics wafting
on icy air, the easy springing strides
of high school runners—boys and girls—as if
autumnal earth becomes a trampoline,
returns each step with "earth power coming"
up in rain with hints of falling snow
and memories from fifty years ago.

Parody of Spring

Varied thrushes work
the autumn garden gone
to seed, their colors
camouflage, blending
with turning leaves, orange,
black, and brown, decay:
parody of bloom.

View of Auke Lake

Orange maple: flame-
like, ignited by
sunlight striking cliff-
sides. Mountains cup
Aladdin's lamp of
endless glacial ice.

Fleet of Mountain Peaks

Fleet of mountain peaks
anchored in a sea of clouds:
Juneau overflight.

All Saints Day (November 1, 2006)

Mallards, motionless
by growing wafers of ice
laced with daybreak mist.

November 10

Ducks blend with gray waves
pulsing toward autumnal shores,
beach foam portending snow.

Gift of Bohemian Waxwings

The gift of an even
    dozen Bohemian
waxwings crowning a tree-
    top, a barren mountain ash,
like fireworks against
    the lead November sky,
harvesting the last of
    crimson berries, when
the single bird explodes
    and all move on.

I think of Rilke
    looking at van Gogh
and how his wheat field
    explodes with crows
against foreboding sky.

Winter Promise

Winter daybreak, crisp,
a hint and promise
of midday sun,
silent, save the sound
of tiny taps on hemlock
that would be raindrops
in another season,
but today the foraging
of unseen winter birds.

New Poems, Part Three:

Congestive Heart Failure:
Letting Go

A triptych in memory of my father,
Leonard Dauenhauer (April 2, 1914–February 7, 2000)

Landscapes of the Heart

Driving past autumnal fields of corn
stalks, naked supplicating trees,
where nature's routes seem clear against the sky,
autumn woods, the understory clear;

the sub-plot—expansive bright decay,
fall colors in the fullest range of brown,
I think how Wallace Stevens always warns
us not to see the barren hardwood trees

as supplicating structures, but the mind
as branching metaphor, dangerous
when unaware and wrought with sentiment.
Yet the heart also needs this landscape

for synapse to beyond, for nervous leaps
of faith, as points of articulation
and comfort, deciduous, with death
protecting life, and nurturing rebirth.

This visit almost certainly our last,
I sense that I am driving into death.
My eyes are sore from crying. How do I tell
you, "It's ok to go now. It's ok."

A Meditation:
Against the Dying of the Light

This late November afternoon I walk
in fading sunlight, savoring the last
warmth of autumn, figuring a route
on eastern fields and hills to keep my face

in light as long as possible, then move
to shade with views of sunset hills stretching
to Vermont, a Cambridge Valley Grandma Moses
scene, then entering the woods by road and game

trail, with slanting winter light oblique
through hardwood forests, feeble beams falling
on remnant rocks of remnant falling walls.
I reach the highest point of wood lot, sit

and meditate on light. How do I tell
my father, "You can go now, it's ok."

A Formal Elegy
(Thinking of Dylan Thomas)

The sunset fields, first dusting snow,
the close of late November day,
I reach the highest point of wood lot,
sit, and meditate on light.

How do I tell myself, despite
the lines proclaiming he should "Not
go gentle into that good night,"

(the Thomist catechism), but
"Rage against the dying of the light,"
when, having reached the final bout,

when time has come to cede the fight
and cut the last connecting knot—
how do I tell him, "It's ok
to go now, it's ok to go."

New Poems, Part Four: Excerpts from the Cycle *Lacrimosa: The Social Web of Cancer*

A Chronology of Grief for Suzie, Rachel, and Tom
in Memory of Ron Scollon (May 13, 1939–January 1, 2009)

> *Ruin hath taught me thus to ruminate,*
> *That time will come and take my love away.*
> *This thought is as a death, which cannot choose*
> *But weep to have that which it fears to lose.*
>
> —William Shakespeare, Sonnet 64

Homage to Po Chü-i

Grown this old, both of us together,
I still wonder what it's like to be old.
. . .
My love for old lost friends thickens
while memories of youth thin away:

there's nothing left but this idle talk,
enough and more for your next visit.
—Po Chü-i, Grown-Old Song,
David Hinton translation

We linger over lines
from Po Chü-i,
a.k.a.
Bai Juyi, who writes
that once you're packed and ready
for your long journey,
it doesn't really matter
if you hang around a while
longer.

The poems come alive,
bring lines
for assisted living,
life lines
from centuries ago,
as old friends visit,

pause for midday naps,
and visit on,
until it's time to go.

Donuts

With in-joke images
of Vonnegut's rolling
donut, a galley full
of slick meat and bad beer,
we joke about going
through the MRI. Warned
of claustrophobia,
we turn it into pleasure,
fantasize our bunks on
fishing boats, dozing
slowly off while chugging
peacefully along,
a trusted skipper
in the wheelhouse. May our
deaths be just as easy
as this preview voyage,
magnetic resonant
Charon ferrying us
to the other shore.

Tough Guy

You should have been dead
two years ago. You stayed
in such good shape that cancer
seemed, in retrospect,
a mild annoyance
until it finally
caught you, like Raven
inside the Whale, eating
everything beyond the point
of no return—the perils
of good health. They tell us
"The healthy have no faith."
But perhaps they're blessed
by not being tested yet.

Approaching Winter Solstice

Due south, December
sunrise. On the radio,
the *New World Symphony*
"going home." If in
the afterlife you meet
Tupou Pulu, please
thank her
for introducing us.
I can't imagine
these thirty years
without you, Suzie,
and the kids. Forgive me
if anything went wrong
as you gather up
to go. Stay
as long as you can.
Leave when you need to.
We'll help you with the bag
you've long since packed.
We'll carry it as far
as customs and security.

Nunc Dimittis

Make haste O God to deliver me!
Make haste to help me, O Lord.
Hear my prayer, O Lord
give ear to my supplications.

—Psalm 69 (70) and 142(3), chanted at the
Orthodox Service of the Parting of the Soul from
the Body, when a person has suffered a long time.

The mode now *nunc*
dimittis, O Lord
now lettest Thou Thy servant
depart in peace.
"'Why can't I die?'
he kept repeating,"
the night-shift report
at new year dawn.

With winter sunrise
New Year's Day
you pass, the old man
gone, as new year
first-born baby boy.
And Eliot, *in my beginning*
is my end, and, *in my end*
is my beginning.

Remembering Ron

—for Ron Scollon (May 13, 1939–January 1, 2009)

You never have to change anything
you get up in the middle of the night to write.
                    —Saul Bellow, as quoted on
                    The Writer's Almanac, June 10, 2009

Why do I wake and get up in the night
with the semi-dream discovery
that you can sing Hart Crane's
"When God lets my body be
with the bulge and nuzzle of the sea"
to the tune of the Navy Hymn,
"Hear us when we cry to Thee
for those in peril on the sea"? Awake,
I know it's e. e. cummings, not Hart Crane
(who did describe "the undinal vast belly"
of the sea). Why dream, then wake to write this?

I guess it's thoughts of you, the urn
with ashes on the bookshelf by the chairs
in which we sat discussing death last summer.
I meditate: how comforting to have
a grave and marker one can journey to
instead of ashes scattered over all
creation. Urn? Not bad, a monument,
a bookend anchoring collected works,
open-ended on your readers' side.

Atonement 2009

—In memory of Ron Scollon (May 13, 1939–January 1, 2009)
Jim Marks (July 21, 1941–February 28, 2009)
Alan Dennis (November 18, 1991–May 6, 2009)
Tag Eckles (May 24, 1950–July 26, 2009)
Linda Marks Dugaqua (September 14, 1946–September 20, 2009)
John Marks (May 11, 1943–September 28, 2009)

Behold, now is the accepted time;
behold, now is the day of salvation;
. . . and as dying, . . . behold, we live.
                    —2 Corinthians 6:2, 9

Death has become like a fog through which one passes
to the sunlit fields of immortality.
                    —St. Nicholas of Zhicha

Displacing juncos and a varied thrush
who forage in the garden gone to seed,
we take the turning fork in hand and dig—
potato harvest, bending to the earth
in slowly lowering autumnal mist
and clouds. At sundown, Yom Kippur begins.
But here and now the sun has been obscure
since summertime, as life continues, about
to be uprooted, for some of us through death—
the inventory once again of friends
and family who died since last I dug
potatoes nearing Yom Kippur, this turning
of the year and of our lives, this litany
of loved ones, multiplied around the world.

We wait in vain for clouds to separate,
for sun to spill again, replacing rain,
as in the growing season. We accept
this day of hidden grace and gifts
in what is otherwise a dismal turning
of the year. Bright against the soil, we take
the gifts and cellar them, and as they grew
and multiplied in summer dark beneath
the earth, our surface darkness and the rain
remind us of our growing season, too.
Renewing all the vows, we hope to leave
a good signature in the book of life.
Late afternoon. Fog dissipates. Fresh snow
in feeble sunlight on the mountainsides.

Basho: Open Road

This open road: no
other traveler; empty
this autumn nightfall.

New Poems, Part Five: Harvesting

Selbst wenn sich der Bauer sorgt und handelt,
wo die Saat in Sommer sich verwandelt,
reicht er niemals hin. Die Erde schenkt.

Even though he cares for it, the grower
never reaches down to where the seed
transforms itself to summer. Earth bestows.
                    —R. M. Rilke, *Sonnets to Orpheus, I. 12*

First Day of Fall

Overcast, autumnal afternoon.
Varied thrush, blending with the last
raspberries. Hummingbird feeders
hang like colored planets in some
science fiction scape, the hummingbirds
themselves long gone, no longer
orbiting, as the northern earth
tilts away from warmth and sunlight
into its polar den. Potatoes
harvested and cellared, garden turned
earlier than usual this year.

Foraging

September morning fog, the foraging
cheeps of chickadees, the splash and clatter
of anchor chains of unseen fishing boats.
Closer in the garden: clearing now.
Gray currants, each berry like a gem
strung on a naked vine. The other
berries memories of summer: raspberries,
strawberries, blueberries, salmonberries;
cherry shrubs too immature to bear.
Birds foraging. The rhubarb going dormant.
But in the garden heart, potato plants
still grow, each yellow, shriveled stalk leading
to hopes of gold below the fog and earth.

Harvesting Potatoes

Nondescript: the autumn
of our lives. A kinglet?
Basking in the spruce top
in fading sun? Juncos
flashier, more lively.
Planted in my rusty
garden chair, I rest while
harvesting potatoes
this crisp September day,
savoring the sunlight
after weeks of steady,
unrelenting rain; rest,
regarding still unturned
potato beds, all those
upright stems of summer
fallen of their age
and weight. Our faith is gold,
of bounty more obscure
beneath the waiting earth.

Digging Spuds

May you live to see your children's children
like olive shoots around your table.
      —Orthodox Wedding Prayer

Nothing gold can stay.
      —Robert Frost

This year, I hoard it for myself,
avoiding all the family kids.
In seasons past I always
coached the growing generations
on harvesting potatoes. Now
greedy for the solitude
to meditate on memories
of those who gave us seed,
too feeble for the energy
of any kids, I dig alone
in guilt, and meditate on life,
somewhere in the moment now
between inheritors and donors,
the time we need to be alone
with our dead, the treasure trove
of life. Below the peaks of mountains
honey-combed with gold mines, I turn
the earth, and gold unfolds by fork-
fuls, nuggets shining in dark soil,
indigenous potatoes, gift
of gardeners now gone, nothing
standard here in shape or size
or uniformity of store-
bought seeds like Yukon Gold or Yellow
Finn; another crop gone feral,
returning to Alaskan earth,
responding in the humid dark
to midnight sun on leaves. If nothing
gold can stay, it can at least
return, returning gold each fall.

October Rain

The reason for living [is] to get ready to stay dead a long time.
—Addie Bundren in
William Faulkner's *As I Lay Dying*

October rain. First, sudden snow come
and gone. Sodden reprieve, performing
all the chores I should have done in June,
July, August, September: now commune
with yard and garden, readying the dead.

With ritual cigar and bourbon straight,
in rusty garden chair I meditate:
is this not typical of life? The scramble?
Eschewing maintenance in bloom, we rush
to make the yard and garden fit for death.

The Tides Forecasting Winter

The world becomes a harp
that gives forth no sound
but in response to the finger of God.
—St. Nicholas of Zhicha

The tides forecasting winter touch
far in- and up-land now, almost
reaching fallow autumn gardens,
the intertidal shallows masked
with the face of the deep: the last
October weekend, when we play
with time in northern latitudes,
adjusting human measurement
to realities of nature.

Fall migration. Rainy, late
October afternoon. I do
my yard work to a varied thrush
and Oregon junco, working
through the yard and garden, blending
with decay in camouflage of
orange, brown, and black, sorting
through what's left beyond the brilliant
bloom of summer, ostentatious
fruits of warmth and sunlight gone
to seed again, as kernels
of the heat and light. We all
prepare, adjust to growing dark.

Potatoes, 2003

On one of few non-rainy afternoons
in waning, low-angle October sun
I dig more horsetail roots than root
crops—potato yield this year the smallest
ever. Always harvesting the season
of atonement, meditating each
pitch-fork turn, with less and less to show:
is this the autumn of my life, body
weakening, most hopes of vernal seed
now manifest, for better or for worse?
I pace myself, the autumn garden still
full of life designed for emptying.
I work along each row, curious, plant
after plant. What will the earth disclose?

Falling in the Garden

is something old men do. My uncle Gus
died in his garden. Once again, the turning
of potatoes and the liturgical
new year for Jews and Orthodox Christians,
new life unearthed with every turning fork.

I meditate on burying our dead,
the friends we lost this year, the rest of us
slowly dying, one way or another.
The endless rains have stopped, the sun briefly
warms the garden—Sunday afternoon, the Feast
of the Birth of the Mother of God, hope
at the harvest turning of the year, like
turning pages of Isaiah, living
out an acceptable year of the Lord.

I use the fork to slowly right myself
again, and one by one examine this
muscle, that bone. I inventory all
my fallen self, accept that I am old,
and take again the turning fork in hand.

Life Support

—in memory of Tag Eckles (May 24, 1950–July 26, 2009)
and Linda Marks Dugaqua (September 14, 1946–September 20, 2009)

We walk by faith, not sight.
             —2 Corinthians 5:7

Rosh Hashanah, potato plants
yellowing in autumnal rain,
the planet slowly turning
liturgically through new year

to atonement, Yom Kippur,
we celebrate the death of friends
and dying of our relatives
and slowly of our selves.

The harvest waits for after rainfall.
The mountains, curtained off
by veils of steady rain,
preserving memories and promises

of sunlight, snowcapped peaks—
an image of the face of God
held in trust, dispersed in glimpses
as much as we can bear to see.

Harvest Festival

—*for friends at Panim Hadashot and Sukkat Shalom*

I
Potatoes 2012:
Sukkot brings no relief—
redundancy of rain
dances, Hosannahs from
deserts of Leviticus
to North Pacific rain
forests. October 1:
postpone the harvest yet
another day, having
missed the only three
September rain-free days
and now officially
the rainy season starts.

II
Festival day three: the rain
stops. 5 AM, the moon
is full, sky clear, and stars
bright in darkness. First
ice on windshields. Fall
is really here. With day-
break, fog settles in. Then sun
filters through the mist
as if through branches on
a desert shelter roof,
bringing to awareness one
by one from mountaintops
to gardens things of earth.

84

III
Sidelined this harvest: hip
replacement imminent.
This year granddaughters, great-
grandchildren take to field
on a treasure hunt for
heritage potatoes.
Moses works his fork, searching
for the fulcrum point
on which to lift and part
the earth, as Elijah
and Sophia vie for
revelations of the
hidden fruits of earth.
Mothers explain the hulls
of springtime seed potatoes
we planted months ago.
The toddler Joshua
and hobbler I observe
the action, his stroller
and my chair astride
a waiting row of hilled
potatoes, as we watch
the harvest kept alive
another generation.

Every Garden Grows One

Every garden, no matter how well tended,
how beautiful, how perfect, how exciting,
is boring. But every garden edge
is something else, where cultivation meets
the wild, and everything that gardeners
reject does well: the compost pile, where lives
we zealous take as weeds repose
and somehow thrive, recycling themselves.

Selected Poems, Part One:
Poems from Little Magazines,
1963–1969

The Pall Bearers

—*in memory of Uncle Fred Grier (July 17, 1889–October 17, 1960)*

One end of the coffin
was carried by his relatives
fitted into the latest styles
by a corps of clerks.
At the other end,
one in checkered socks
and hunting coat,
the other in a double-breasted suit
he'd been sold years ago,
both in sport shirts,
wide, wide ties, and baggy pants,
were his friends.

Ukrainian Flirtation Dance

I dance prisidka at her feet.
Her skirt sways above her calves;
her knees play with its hem
as thighs press up; then feet in soft red boots
push away the floor. She caresses air,
and smiles with dancing eyes and tongue-moist lips.
Young breasts lift and hover
above the stillness of her hips.
I dance prisidka at her feet;
bright ribbons stream from her hair.
Details of her hand-stitched blouse
blur in streaks of red on white.
Prisidkas noticed, open arms await
my hands, dirty from slapping dusty boots.
And I dance prisidka at her feet.

At the Spring: Glasby Pond, Fall 1963

I turn my hunting hat around, and in push-up, lay
a bridge of me across the spring's moat of soggy leaves.
Hinged toes and granite-pressing fingertips
lower me to drink my silhouette.
I leave my halo, passing mirrored sky.
Seeing in my shadow what must lie
preserved and fruitful in the spring, I set
my mouth so that no slightest ripple slips,
and, weighted by a breath of current, cleaves
the sifting tiers of intricate decay.

Uncle Martin, 1963

—in memory of Martin Dauenhauer (1877–1967)

The old man lay in traction all
summer watching weeds grow
and city me learn his tractor
clutch, tooling down the rows
of corn beyond his falling
barn. We both knew I was no
paradigm of farming. I
had cultivated German, he
the earth of New York State.

In modern terms, a teenage
runaway, he bought a farm he turned
blue chip. Aging, he disposed
of unused edges, so his farm
fit better than his clothes. His land
and half the banks in Syracuse
provided interest rates for life.
Suburbanites in subdivided
yards soon found his house against
their ranch house grain, and so the whole
development was questioning
whoever let the farmer in.

Now relatives urge progress. Even he
admits he likes the TV set
beside the growing pile of daily
papers for his outhouse. He'd had
a telephone put in, could modernize
a call for help. In traction now,
the last farmer in the family
watches hired pickers, listens
to nephews urging convalescence
in the city. I leave them, walk
out past his rat-filled barn, long since
emptied of its cows. I wander
through the orchards—apples, cherries—
return through berry gardens, then
his vineyard, tasting fruits of his
weed-moated world: the lush and dusty,
tart-skinned grapes the pickers missed.

Tootsie

—in memory of Bertha Dauenhauer
(September 15, 1902–May 21, 1982)

Tootsie: the childhood
photograph, the farm girl
with apple blossom eyes
feeding geese. A life

dried like last year's
apples. A cash crop,
the harvest always seemed
for someone else; the labor

ended in preserves. Your lamp
was always polished, wick
trimmed, waiting; yet the bridegroom
somehow never came. Summer dust

settled in the vineyard. Grapes
were harvested; your parents
crushed and pressed them, but the wine
mothered. They hoarded life
until it couldn't grow.

Thought and Memory:
Finland, Summer 1963

My rowboat glides on soft, black lake
as I ship oars and watch a raven make
his way homeward over shaggy trees
to Valhalla, to report of everything he sees.

Viewing him, imagination caught
and linked my shoulders of memory and thought
with a head like Odin's, as I saw at last
this remnant of an omnipresent past.

Neva Farm (Finland, 1963)

We cross the hayfields gleaned by morning work,
and, horse in hand, approach your ancient farm,
hungry as the wolves that used to lurk
in winter nights. Log buildings, arm in arm,

link inward, still defending wolfen times. Inside,
you wove the rugs that warm the wooden room.
You'll seat me at your oldest bench with pride,
opposite the oven and the loom,

and serve me milk and fresh, wood oven bread.
But, chosen from the doors we had ahead,
the formal sitting room is bid instead.

Berrying (Finland, 1963)

Without a touch of sugar—bitter sweet,
or sweet alone, or bitter by themselves,
you varied day by day your berry treat
from swamp or meadow edge, or from the shelves

of forest rock; knew where to go and when to wait
for tastes and memories you anticipate.

I learned from you how simple things enchant:
berries I can't translate, or transplant.

Ilmatar: Finland, 1966

I am driven by my longing
and my understanding urges.
—*Kalevala*, First Rune (Kirby translation)

Drilling, where the tree
roots stop; drilling
where tractor tires rest
on granite knees, again
undressed; now his
labor shapes the land.

His morning's work—now vases
where spruce boughs flag
places to be planted
with dynamite. And pressing
his compressed-air drill,
his mind acts, his brain
thinks in a two-hand, obscene,
fertile Finnish finger gesture
beneath the sky and water flag.

Full Moon: Finland, 1966

No more the magic
candlelight of fir

trees, or Eichendorf's
kraut romantic soul
flying home on moonbeams,

but you still make her blood
and my desire flow.

Housewife (Finland, 1967)

"A perfect friendship. Death.
A search for immortality, that fails."

You do the supper dishes. We discuss
the tedium of Christian afterlife.

You flee to *Gilgamesh*. You talk
of rotting in the ground. Life:

like Bede's sparrow, flying through the hall,
a brief feasting between the dirty dishes

you wash and wash again before they break—
dishes, with their cuneiforms of rice.

Dust: A Poem on Translation

(after reading Nelly Sachs's German translations
of the Finland-Swedish poet Edith Södergran)

Now, so easy.
Light and weightless,
the language of her song
settles on your own.

The burning
is over.
The heated nights,
the dry eyes at dawn;

the hunger
is past,
the trembling hands,
the stomach pain;

the clash of culture:
smashing
of sculptured lines and crystal
images.

The beautiful,
so easy now.
Light and weightless,
settles on your own.

Three Texas Poems for Loyd Mowry
(Sinologist, among other things)

1. Texas

in the lime dust, by the
powdered-white
cactus,
the sun
like a white
chicken
moves across the yard

2. Hill Climb

when spring comes,
i take my motorcycle
& go riding

loyd mowry
in a chinese painting:
huge mountains
& misty writing

3. Mowry in Brownsville

mowry in brownsville:
chinese writing in the corner
of a huge state of things

Sketches of Big Bend:
West Texas, Easter Weekend 1966

1. Blow-out

Holy Thursday, 1966
    '57 Ford
blow-out at 80
    on the Pecos River bridge
so, watching tires
    and dashboard dials,
we roll along
    through leopard hills
and pace a freight
    to Sanderson.

2. Ghost Town: Haunting Sounds

Terlingua: rusted bed springs, busted
glass, bottles, tin cans litter sunlit
Sonoran desert floor in midday heat.

Terlingua: hum of bumblebees
droning through the open
adobe doors
in prickly-pear Terlingua,
ocotillo, broken
century-plant-
agave-stalk Terlingua.

3. Road to Presidio

By the road to Presidio,
against a desert hillside:
adobe houses, a shiny,
bright-red pickup truck.

Two Wisconsin Poems:
Madison, Fall 1967

colder now, your nose
runs and yr hands
freeze on the handlebars
of yr bike: october

fine mist on my glasses
riding home

november
snowflakes
falling on the marsh

on the lake: mallards
in snowfall and water, patterns
framed in field-
glasses, with ever-changing focus
of black and white

Listening to a Lecture on Zola
(Madison, Wisconsin, Fall 1967)

—for Anne Krooth and Betsy Edelson

The establishment professor of
upper- or upper-middle-class origins imparting
liberal establishment academic ideas to
establishment liberal and/or
conservative students of
upper or upper middle class origins:

"There were nicer neighborhoods
Zola could have
observed. He is wrong to view
his lower class slum workers as
indicative of
the human condition."

The professor rejects
Zola's idea
of environment providing
predictable results.

Two Poems on the War in Vietnam, Madison, 1967

1. The Missing Link

The missing link between animals and real
human beings is most likely ourselves.
—Konrad Lorenz

Sleeping on my lap, our kittens: purring
infant bodies, far from jungles, whirring
helicopters, soldiers warring
for the minds of men
and the bodies of women.

Every bullet is a seed maturing.

2. Conversion

—for the little kids in my old neighborhood
who are being gutted by hand grenades in Vietnam

I read these entrails: man
is full of shit. His insight—
eyeballs, hanging on his cheeks
like tears. And what are words but visions
of soldiers of the past, plucked
by the vultures before we see them.

I read the entrails. Helicopters
fly their bodies home.

Bread Lines

We feed our depression of ducks.

Like marines, they wade to the shore,
but the ducks have forgotten their killing

and come to St. Francis of Auschwitz,
a sissy with chemical bread;

they come to the governing hand,

and St. Francis cringes in terror
aghast at innocent eyes,

dropping his presents of mind in the web
his footprints will leave in the sand.

My Last Metaphor

Stars in their eyes,
the blueblood and lily white
fingers of the faceless bureaucrats
search their files:

our flag is bloody fingers
indexing the world.

Four Perspectives

1.
Reaching out
to get the sunlight.

2.
Because the sunlight causes elongation
of the cells on the far side
of the trunk.

3.
Because the cells located on the
dark side of the tree grow longer,
bending the tree toward
sunlight and emptiness
of the canopy level at the
center of the marsh.

4.
That these trees extend
over the edges
of the sunny marsh.

From This Perspective

From this perspective, and in this
light, the run-off of the first
heavy spring rain down the
black elm trunk

is like a spotted
snake. But from no perspective
is this slow and constant pulse
of white bubbles meta,

for the eye is strained
from being taught to see
everything
in terms of something else.

First Phenology

(Madison, March 27, 1969, 11:45 AM)

No pattern
imposed on snow drops
melting from the back porch
roof: dot–
dash intersections
of water and sunlight
as which they are seen.

Definition of Itself

(Madison, Wisconsin)

It is enough that
this perfect oak leaf
is melting through the ice
and resting
in a perfect, two-inch-deep,
sheer-ice wall outline
of itself,
under a quarter-inch of
clear ice water
symbolic of nothing.

Field Guide: Madison, Wisconsin

—for Jerry Evans

Listen, how the words flourish
as we walk the finite paths
between the fields of infinite events

of lupine, spiderwort, and shooting star;
of birdsfoot-trefoil, Indian
paintbrush, blue-eyed grass,

puccoon; of prairie-dock to come
and spring ephemerals gone beneath the shade.
We stop, match names of things

to what is here, and listen, now
how after we have passed, the plants
revert to seeds and syllables.

Selected Poems, Part Two:
from *Phenologies*

We awake in the same moment to ourselves and to things.
                            —Maritain (by way of George Oppen)

Let's see the very thing and nothing else
. . . without evasion by a single metaphor.
                            —Wallace Stevens, "Credences of Summer"

   —for Sandy with fond memories of cribbage at break-up being one way of
   sorting out what's in the cards, and dealing with "Reluctance" to "accept
   the end of a love or a season."

   and with memories of Yksi, Gray Man, Pumpkin, Basil, and Timmy; Kaksi,
   who never got to make the trip; and Trixie, a.k.a. Mutzoid, who survived
   it all.

January: silence
and the tapping of
chickadees on birch,
the crunch
of boots on snow.

Conceptions of Snow

Underfoot: snyek,
snyek; skiing
schnee and first–
falling
snow.

Snowshoe partitive:
lumi, lunta.
Scene in sounds:
dleit.
Neige.

Nyezh–
no? No,
never:
as un–
sound, as
con–
ception
of the snow.

Nuances of Dawn

Morning Star
over Soldotna,
cow moose still
where bedded down at dusk
on the frozen
Kenai River.
I think of Williams,
Wallace Stevens,
and archetypes of dawn
at twenty-five below.

January 10:
twenty below, two moose
on the homestead road,
Orion over McHugh Peak,
Telemann Concerto
in B-flat Major;
woodstove at full roar,
car battery on the table
by the oil stove.

Thoughts While Bringing
in Firewood, January 17

1
Cold night, Orion
rising over Flattop by
quarter moon; cold, but
colder down below in
Anchorage, at minus thirty-five
with no
security of wood.

2
Reports from the Interior:
how people keep
oil drums on the stove
to keep the stove oil
warm enough to flow.

3
Reports from the Interior:
how wonderful
silence feels
at seventy below.

Winter Walk

Recalling now
that moment in Wisconsin
on a winter walk, our path
met the line of tiny
animal tracks, straddled
here and there by brush marks
till they stop:
this must record some
wing tips touching snow.

"Pome" for Larry & Beth Beede
(February 11, 1970)

The pattern of the day
was lavender klister
on brown skis on
snow, redpolls
as plentiful that day
as sunlight dripping
from the black spruce.

March 8,
winter morning at ten or twelve below:
driving down the mountain
into work,
passing all the dogs
left behind at school bus stops.

March and
oil's run out, the road
far too drifted over
for any truck.

Wednesday, April 2:
sawing firewood from
blowdown; first Canada geese
flying north over Flattop.

April 12, annual blizzard
one month late this year;
sipping toddies and VO,
digging Jelly Roll
Morton as winds die down,
and it softly snows
all afternoon
all evening
into dark.

April 13:
hauling water by snowshoe
over chest-high drifts.

May 6:
light snow
falling from the fog.

May 11:
after winter, after
April and May
snow, I had forgotten
the smell and sound and feel
of light rain
falling in the trees and
Flattop socked in.

May 15
spring evening, splitting firewood:
concepts created
when we name these sounds of things
carried on the air,
like first marmot whistles
from up-canyon
still-snowy slopes.

Sunday, May 16:
at treetop level,
a marsh hawk overhead
banks and glides away,

but focus and f-stops
are set for a golden-crowned
sparrow on the woodpile.

May 20, Anchorage:
the first time this year
for ozone smell and puffs
of raindrops in the dust.

May 22, snowing:
in a soggy clearing
last-fall bear scat
in the mist; marmot whistle
and the calls
of four different birds
I always have to learn again
each spring.

Late May
again, still day-
light after 10 PM,
my paper lit
from snow on mountainsides;
working on these poems
until too dark to see.

Driving home at 4 AM in June
from working on a Tlingit manuscript,
I discover I have lived my life thus far
without discovering the fragrance
of alder and of mountain ash
blossom after light
Alaska rain.

Earthquake

Falling from a birch leaf,
how the impact of a single
raindrop on a single
blade of grass
shakes the earth.

Magnificat

How the lens of rain-
drop magnifies the blade of
grass: magnificat.

So much
really *does* depend
on the wheelbarrow
in particular;
in this case, home-made,
second-hand, and rusty,
the metal wheel
hanging on by wire,
filled with rainwater,
and a Wilson's warbler
on the good handle.

mountain-
    side
        summer
long
    sun
        sets
golden
    crowned
        sparrow
Rabbit
    Creek
        rush
golden
    crowned
        sparrow
all
    night
        long

August 8

grass and fireweed
over my head now
as I walk the trail
looking for our cat.

Someday he will wander off,
never seen again:
The Little Gray Man,
debonair,
hunter and lover
par excellence.

Driving to Alaska

The tiny animals we've killed
on summer highways, their small
bodies and tiny genitals
still warm, and carrying
food home in their mouths:
how tenuous
existence is.

August evening, ten o'clock:
on the high peaks fog-mist
rolling in, covering the still
unmelted snow;

walking up the hillside
from latrine site, lantern light
in the sauna window
and the open door;

darkening now
even in Alaska.

August, but the archetypes of October:
dampness, and the driving rain.

Sipping Seagrams to chamber music,
Beethoven, *Archduke Trio*,
working on manuscripts,
watching it pour.

Hiking in the Kenai Peninsula

Across the valley and
straight out now, the three
sheep and one
black bear

on this side
marmot whistle and ptarmigan flock
and, hand over hand now,
a fresh marmot turd
crowberry black, sticky
to the touch, but
odorless.

Labor Day

1
Splitting firewood: first
snowflakes settle in my ears
and on the chopping block.

2
Sudden blizzard, moving up-canyon
from across the Inlet and Alaska Range:
the earth white within an hour.
We stoke the woodstove and,
sipping Scotch, watch it snow
and slowly melt.

3
Next morning
waken to the stove door clank
and a friend's footsteps
crunching frozen earth
between the woodpile
and the house:
Labor Day, September
1970.

September 5:
when fog lifts
there is snow.

Late September: stars
are out again; after
midnight sun, I had forgotten
the stars, even
Orion, Pleiades.

Exactitude

Gray Man, the second
of our five cats, is
sleeping all curled up
on the inter-folded flaps
of a Lucky Lager four
six-pack cardboard case
in which I keep my
dissertation: my
scholarly appa-
ratus, all caved in.

Auto Repair

In sunlight
silver wrenches
on black flooring
with the first golden leaf
fallen from the birch.

September 27,
walking to the highway:
the sound of frozen leaves
falling to the ground.

Sunday, October 4,
9:25 AM
the sun rises
over Flattop
and suddenly floods
the woodstove corner
of the living room
and my reading chair
with light.

Dogs barking
in full moonlight
middle of the night:
neighbors' dogs outside,
ours inside, barking:
cats out of bed
leaping to windowsills.

We later learn
nothing turns them on like this
but bear. But now

there is no
snow for tracking:
we will never know
what passed us in the night,
October 1970.

Morning Walks

1
October
eleven years ago—
Berlin, 1959—
walking to a German school.
How strange now,
walking with my dog
on the frozen homestead road:
October in the foothills
of the Chugach Range.

2
It's cold enough:
the stream is partly frozen,
lacy, where the road
dips beneath it.

3
On morning walks, the road
snow-white, black-cut
by water at the ford.

October: splitting wedge
cold now to the touch
on frosty nights. The sounds:
kindling, as it parts, curling
from the axe head and
tinkles to the frozen ground: Coleman
lantern hiss, and now and then
coyote calls
from up-canyon
where the snow has stayed.

October 17, at dusk
after hooking up the oil, at last
we first hear the hooting
of the Great horned owl.

October 21,
early afternoon:
hiking up the canyon,
following bear tracks
until they fill
with falling snow.

Late Afternoon,
Alaska Methodist University Campus

Sunday: gray; the scrape
of hockey skates, slap-
shot crack, puck-thud
on backyard boards.

A walk from sunset
downhill into darkness
where at well below
freezing, people tar
their skis: huddled
silhouettes in garage
doorways, with the blue
torchlight warming
bare hands,
tar, and wood.

Autumn Tune-up

A gray day
of men in coveralls,
birds working
barren treetops,
the sound of chickadees
above the soft
clicking and the whirr
of socket wrench.

Sapphic Moonrise, Flattop Mt.

Neck stiff, cold,
cramped when I came out of it.
How long had I been standing
in the mountain road
staring at the moon
in ecstasy of stasis?

A stasis of ecstasy—
her images: forever
pressed and rising
flowers of the grass
lifting in coda
to the dancing feet of girls
circling an altar, rising
to full moon rise
twenty-five
centuries ago.

❧❧

Full moon, November 3.
That time of year again:
car parked facing downhill
as far up as we can drive;
walking uphill more, then
walking side hill home
through boot-top-high
October snow.
Moon over Flattop;
across the canyon,
across the sky,
over McHugh Peak: Mars.

November, any year:
by three o'clock the need
for artificial light; light
the lamp, continue
reading, writing.

Turn the wick down
low, to start it burning
char from the mantle.
Full moon
rising over Flattop
floods the den,
casting a shadow
of the lamp itself
across the moonlit
manuscripts
scattered on the desk.

November 15:
I want to use this paper
for a poem, but discover
this scribbled phenology

dated October—barren
trees and gray land;
you say it makes you think
of owls and field mice.

Evening, December 1: Orion
climbing over Flattop.
Take the old
battery inside
so the jeep will start
by morning star.

It didn't.

Winter now:
using the woodstove
to supplement the oil.

**December 21, eight-
thirty**: up
before daybreak,
cats and dog fed,
writing by kerosene,
watching the blizzard
dawn, thinking of
Pasternak
writing winter poems
with winter finished
before his poetry.

December 31
approaching midnight.
Silence.
The sound alone
of my down parka
being lightly fallen on
by snowflakes.

Selected Poems, Part Three: from *Glacier Bay Concerto*

—For Nora:
   Raven Woman, Child of the Clan of Grass

   You handed me my life, as from a bookshelf,
      blowing off the dust.
                  —Boris Pasternak

Glacier Bay Concerto
First Movement:
Commander Glass Cuts Deeper into Kake

1

I like your stuff, Frost, but I often wish
you'd stuck to maple trees. The gift
outright, but not yet quite:
the Organic Act of 1884
so Whites could take and transfer
title to their claims; the Homestead
Act of '98, so squatters'
deeds got recognized; the Indian
Allotment Act of 1906
let Tlingits claim
whatever land was left.
The Indians made citizens
in 1924. And finally
(December 18, 1971)
the Alaska Native Claims
Settlement Act, making Alaska
Natives into profit-making
corporations. The land
was theirs before they were the land's.
And parenthetically, the deed
of gift was many deeds of war.

3
1675
Philip among the first:
wife and son
sold as slaves
to the West Indies
by the Pilgrim Fathers.
1619
the Massachusetts lose
ninety percent to smallpox;
1620
the Pilgrim Fathers claim
the Massachusetts fields
(now fallow)
and have the first Thanksgiving
with Massasoit the Chief
and pass the death penalty
for refusal to be Christian.
Massasoit's successor,
his first son Alexander,
dies from interrogation
at the Pilgrim hands.
His second son, (op. cit.) Philip,
gets his head impaled by Pilgrims
in Plymouth on a pike.

4

Sez Levi-Strauss, look
for myth in our society
in politics, not
mythology; to wit, the
separation of church and
state, but not of
religion and politics.
Writes John Winthrop
1634
"the natives are neare all dead
of the small poxe, so as the Lord
hathe cleared our title
to what we possess."
The higher use of the land:
from Plymouth to Yakutat
illiterate savages
blocking the path
of civilization,
illiterate savages,
children of the Devil.

14
1869
General Jeff Davis
(no relation
to the great one),
Captain Richard Meade,
the army and the navy,
level Kake.
"Nothing was left to be done
except to burn their villages,
which I ordered to be done,"
writes Jeff Davis
to the War Department
and the *New York Times*.
Jeff Davis:
rumor has it
got away with murder
back in Tennessee
before they made him
ruler of Alaska.
General Jeff Davis
(no relation
to the great one).
Early 1870s
Davis is promoted
to the Modoc wars,
and gets a street
named after him
in Sitka.

30
1882
the U.S. Navy, the
bombing of Angoon:
canoes on beaches shattered
by Gatling gun,
the village shelled,
a landing party loots
then burns it to the ground.
Only two houses
left standing.

42
Rednecks in Yakutat:
"Look, the goddamned Indians
think it's ok
to live on moose and fish;
they don't give a damn
about development;
it's a goddamned waste
the way they want it.
The whole country
should be turned over
to people who can make
something out of it."
(*Seattle Post Intelligencer*
October 26, 1975)

47
Update: *Anchorage
Daily News*, Friday
May 4, 1979;
Rep. Steven Symms
(R–Idaho) says,
"If Alaska's energy
and mineral resources
are not permitted to be
exploited, Americans
will someday be sending boys
over to the Persian Gulf
to die
for a barrel of oil."

55
Alaska Airlines
flight 66
jet service for
Cordova, Yakutat,
and Juneau.

Welcome to the Great
Land: Cordova, crew–cut
tourists, big game
hunters, construction
workers getting off.

Eyak language,
three speakers left
whose hearts have grown old,
whose speech will die forever
and the instance
of human voice
crystallize to text,
a lexicon, and grammar.

The trumpeter swans
linger to November,
floating at Eyak Lake
between the ice and waterfall.
They will build among no rushes.
We will wake
finding they have flown away.

59
At the rise and set
of every era,
the silhouette
of sky and land,
sun and earth,
the forest of symbols,
the red
and the black.

Glacier Bay Concerto
Second Movement:
The Woman in the Ice

Sorrow silenced the harps
of the children of Zion
for they sang not
among strangers.
> —St. Cosmas, *Nativity Canon*

A Reading of *Persephones*
(for Nathaniel Tarn in Alaska)

5
We see now
how everything
is metaphor and true:
Jesus and Orpheus,
whose bodies are instruments,
whose poems are
creation of the world.
"He lord of song whose lyre
is of his sinews and of his sufferings
compounded."

6

We mature with poetry,
with songs of vision
and experience;
we raise these questions
so that myth
will mean for us:
questions of the body
and the blood;
of blood guilt
and redemption,
creation, and the word,
of death and immortality—
Jesus and Orpheus,
torn apart and eaten,
the sons of man,
as are we all, and all
children of God.

Shaawat Séek': The Daughter of Woman

Lord, you are our God, even as you were the God
of Abraham and Sarah, the God of our fathers and mothers,
the God of all the ages of Israel.
They are our past as we are their future.
—Prayer at Rosh Hashanah

1
Everyone with grandfather
rights but the owners,
all trace removed
by glaciers and government,
all trace removed
but eternal memory,
remembrance of them
from generation to generation,
living memory and knowledge
of the woman in the ice
that each generation
praises to another, composing
poetry anew, saying
worthy are you
to claim the land
for you remained
and purchased with your blood
redemption for your people
and redemption for the children
of the Clan of Grass:
Shaawat Séek'
Daughter of Woman
who sealed it with her blood.

2
Experience,
the theme of which is blood
and blood guilt acceptance.
The data: a girl at puberty
and the power of the first
passage of her blood.
Kaasteen, secluded. Woman
but still a child, cries
in loneliness, cries
from seclusion
for the company of ice.
And the ice advanced, the village
emptied, driven to
canoes—all the people
for the sake of one:
Chookaneidí,
the People of the Grass,
whose people knew
and one came forward
to stay behind,
and entered into ice:
Shaawat Séek'
the Daughter of Woman
who entered once
for all,
for all the people
of the Clan of Grass
and all their seed, the Children
of the Clan of Grass,
by her own blood
having obtained
eternal redemption.

3
Shaawat Séek'
the Woman in the Ice
who understood
without the shedding of blood
there is no forgiveness,
who understood
it is impossible
for the blood of animals
to take away sins,
who understood
retreat, who knew
whoever tries
to keep a life
will lose it;
whoever loses it
preserves a life
forever; who knew
the ice would stop
but never the moving
ice of obligation;
to mediate now
the past and future,
time profane
and time eternal
humanity and ice.

4
The future built
on dying generations:
like every act of love,
like every sentence
of human speech,
the salmon runs,
and Shaawat Séek'
the Daughter of Woman
and the child of man.

New Anny

9
Cape Spencer:
we used to stop there
if the tide was right.
The gumboots
were just like fruit.
They were so juicy
you could eat them
right off the beach.
Juicy things.

We trolled
all along there.
We dried fish there.
We had two
smokehouses.
There used to be
two villages there.

10
Dundas Bay:
that's where you'd roll around
in berries
'til you smelled
like berries.
It smelled good.

We used to go to patches
where no matter where you stepped,
you'd crush strawberries.

When we'd go back to the boat,
you'd smell of it for days.

12
The only thing
I wish they'd taken off
was the wheel.
You should have seen
the wheel
of *New Anny*.
It was a work of art.
My father and Uncle Jimmy
built it
out of yellow cedar.
It was so strong
I could stand on it.
I used to stand
on the handles
and make it turn.
It's gone now.
Gone.
My father got too old
and sold it.
Then it sank.
New Anny
gone forever,
lost at sea.

Rilke at Glacier Bay

Lest the land grow desolate
you will always hear our voices on it.
　　　　　—Aant'iyéili, Lukaax̱.ádi composer

1
In the beginning
was the word,
and the ice descended: pure
transcendency,
establishing a temple
in "to hear."

2
And it must
be heard.
O God,
this is so
ephemeral.
As the word
passes
so the utterance,
the sentence,
the need for interaction,
human life,
speech,
and language
itself.

3
The utterance
gives it life.
There is no
return.
There is only
invocation
of the instance
as time becomes
the thing itself
like the dancer
and the dance,
like the speaker
and the speech,
the words uniting
the living and the dead,
the words creating
the world of metaphor,
breaking the bonds
and profanity of time.

4
The language
eternal
though the speech
extinct.
As every utterance
brings language to life
through speech,
that very speech,
the instance of speech
that gives it life,
is the passing of speech.
As the sentence closes,
it brings the spoken language
closer to death.

5
Language as the birth
of dying generations.
The language lives
though the speakers die
'til death removes
the final instance
of human speech
from the cycle of being born
and there is no more;
death by death
the instance giving way
to eternal structure,

eternal memory:
death by death
the concrete event
moribund,
bound by death
to the abstraction
of eternal life.

6
The speech recedes
like Glacier Bay
emptied of its people,
emptied of its soul
except the sole
woman in the ice
whose voice we hear,
whose voice of silence
creates her own
eternal words
of requiem.

Mt. Fairweather: Tsalxaan

1
Sunlight
sparkles on the water,
every flash the brilliance
of a famous man.

Like Lee
going to the mountains,
Tsali
coming down,
and Davidson:
> *Was it for this*
> *we stacked our arms*
> *obedient*
> *to a soldier's trust?*
> *Was I betrayed?*
> *Did I betray?*
From Widukind to Vlassov
trails of tears.

2
And as for people,
their days are like the grass;
they bloom
like fireweed.
When autumn winds have passed,
they are no more,
and their own land
no longer knows them.
They have blossomed
into seed.

3
In a Glacier Bay Concerto:
ice moving
like the footsteps
of a thousand mourners,
a continuum
to kittiwakes and terns.

4
Your tears burst,
Child of the Clan of Grass,
streaming on a text:
your fathers' song.

Your tears fall
on the very words
of kinship that create them.

Your grief is passage,
admission through the door
that cannot be shut
for you have not
denied their name.

5
I will lift up my eyes
to the mountains
where my help
is from.
While sunlight sparkles
on summer water
and snowcapped peaks,
history is now
and Glacier Bay.

Glacier Bay Concerto
Third Movement:
Raven Woman, Child of the Clan of Grass

*"Nein," sagte der Zwerg. "Lasst uns vom Menschen reden!
Etwas lebendiges ist mir lieber als alle Schätze der Welt."*
—Brüder Grimm, "Rumpelstilzchen"

*"No," said the dwarf. "Let us talk about people! Something
alive is dearer to me than all the treasures of the world."*
—Brothers Grimm, "Rumpelstilzchen"

Autumn at Sheldon Jackson College

Sitka September:
wet wool smell
of halibut coats
after a week
of heavy rain.

October:
Eskimos in ponchos
in the gray rain, then

that moment when
after four-day rain,
herring gulls swarm
to harbor, black
against the clearing sky, and

Sitka after the storm:
kelp in floating sunlight
on the high tide.

Two Fog Poems

Composed by Genesis (age 2) and Elena (age 4) aboard the MV *Le Conte*, Lynn Canal, Sunday, September 26, 1976

Is that white a fire
or a waterfall?

It looks like rice water
where the fog
is pouring in the ocean.

The Fruits of Winter

These are the fruits of winter.
Orchards of Sitka spruce
boughs heavy with snow
ripen of their weight and

tumble into baskets
of snowbound grass,
picked by the touch of vision
in a harvest of being seen

at winter midnight, with the moon
itself a snowball
like an apple sliced in half.

Walking the Sitka harbor
late at night,
watching the snow
settle on halibut boats
and water;

composing a Rilke translation
I should have finished
long ago.

Winter Ferry: Haines to Juneau

No planes
will fly today.
The gray sky joins
the ocean gray, the weather always
just out of reach, dissolving
just beyond the bow
as if the ship
allows the fog to keep
its proper distance,
as if the fog
parts to let it through,
as if this weather—
snowfall
sifting from the fog,
melting on the water—
has courted ships
and fenced with them
for ages.
The *Matanuska*,
lounges emptied now
of tourists:
a winter afternoon,
the sound of Tlingit spoken
softly in the darkness;
moving slowly
into night and snow.

Raven, after the Storm

1
Winter storm:
with every step, Raven
shoulder deep in snow.

2
A black leaf
skitters on snow crust
but Raven
caves it in.

3
Raven,
trying to pivot
on a fulcrum
of collapse.

4
Raven
up to his ass
in snow.

In Tlingit,
núkwdi háatl'i
ptarmigan turds:
enormous snowflakes
that fall in March.

❧❧

Sitka koan: it rains,
but you don't get wet;
it hails,
but you don't get hit.

❧❧

As if all
Sitka were in flames:
the white, blinding glare
of sunlight after rain
on black shingle roofs
steaming
in the sun,
complete with Raven—
winking,
iridescent Phoenix
hopping on the roof.

For Sy and Chris

Tending their gardens,
the counterculture
following the fish
from Tenakee,
Tlingit youth
trolling with tape decks
    Hey boys
    take me back
    I wanna ride in Geronimo's
    Cadillac
get enough fish
to break even
after food and gas;

and the Harvard Tlingits
home for the summer,
home to the cannery,
packing salmon eggs
for Japan:
XIP
Excursion Inlet Packing
summer '74.

For the Upikson Girls

"Are you Wolf
or Crow?"

"I'm
Eskimo!
I'm a Boeing
747!"

The Ramification of Aries

Is this
the crestfallen hero
of the new era?
The hunter and gatherer
of subsistence
grantsmanship?
"What have you done
to preserve your heritage?"
asks the man
of Andrew Hope the Third
who replies,
"I slept. I fed myself,
I washed my face,
brushed my teeth. . . ."
(Oral tradition.)
This may be the true
metaphysical juice
of Krishna Consciousness:
what do you get when you cross
an eagle and a snail?

Pneuma:
A Family Poem for Leni and Boboy

Leni
sounds the letters out:
"M-y-s-t-i-c-s a-n-d
Z-e-n M-a-s-t-e-r-s
b-y T-h-o-m-a-s M-e-r-t-o-n."
Our grandson
takes it up and says
"I'm Grampa Dick,"
thumbing through the book
and fanning it, enjoys
the wind it makes
blowing on his face.

You whisper,
"This is breath:
the breath
of your book."

If Thomas Merton,
both Suzukis,
and Hui Neng were alive,
I'd send them each
a copy of this poem.

For Marcia, Dawn, Joel, and Rachel

Framed in birches, children
playing in the sun, in rainbows
of garden hose water;
August afternoon sunlight
haloing the leaves, showering
sparkles on the grass, on faces,
hair and swimsuits: bodies
jump rope with a stream
of water, these last pre-
adolescent days, these last
days of summer, as if watering
a garden of images forever
planted in the mind, starter
images, a garden
of little girls.

Marissa

Snow falling on Sitka
spruce, like genealogy: infinity
passing through these
2.61
acres, evenly on housetops,
the woodpile, a snowman, children
playing in the snow, and you—
fifth generation, fourth
living generation on this land
riding metal horseback,
swinging in your grandma's and your great-
grandmother's view, marking
time like a pendulum in this grandfather's
clock of falling snow.

It's difficult
to type your manuscripts.
Each word makes me pause
and think about the Raven
who transcribed them, whose little
footprints on the page
this writing is.

Raven woman,
Child of the Clan of Grass
standing on the beach
in sunlight:
how fine you are.

Selected Poems, Part Four:
from *The Shroud of
Shaawat Séek'*

Lullaby for Ḵaat'eix̱
(Myths & Texts for Katrina Marie)

How rare to be born a human being!
—Gary Snyder

Katrina, Yekaterina, the Great
Martyr Catherine, died
and risen again, borne
by her Godmother. (Mary,
we knew you wouldn't stay
away for long!) Katrina,
what a morning! Sleep now,
rest, having descended
into water, crushed the heads
of dragons who lurk there in Viking
serpentine, your Norwegian blood
buoyant. Like Beowulf, you battled
all the powers of evil
and emerged, Tlingit woman warrior,
victorious, to walk forever
in the newness of life.

Four Sketches

1. Hoonah

Hoonah,
where even snow machines
perch like ravens
looking backward
over their shoulders
with eyes
of dashboard dials.

2. Memorial for Willie Marks

In a sea of salmon
the Porpoise Ladies surface
and disappear,
distributing their gifts
like flashes of memory.

3. The Shroud of Shaawat Séek'

—for all departed Chookaneidí and their relatives

On days like this—
the land of Glacier Bay a brilliant
shroud of powder snow
and rainbow clouds—
the sun shines through, forever
evaporating grief.

4. Family Birthday Picnic, Auke Bay
Sunday, June 9, 1984

As if composing
on the book of life,
the single porpoise
moves closer to the shore.
Its dorsal fin,
an element or cursor,
returns on scrolling lines
of waves.

Hoonah Graves

*—In Memory of Jim Nagatáak'w Marks
and Eliza Marks*

From the grave house
with its mossy roof,
the brown bear rises,
facing out to sea.

A pair of whales
blowing, breaching, diving,
curves across the surface
like thread and needle, as
if beading a design
on the empty felt
of memory and sea.

The final dive: flukes,
empty bear paws,
November rain.

Selected Poems, Part Five: from *Frames of Reference*

—for my father
   and in memory of my mother

We live in eternity
while we live in time.
It is only by imagination
that we know this.
                    —Wendell Berry

The Present is the point at which time touches eternity.
                    —C. S. Lewis

The entrance of eternal life
being ever in that Moment
which separates past and future.
                    —Alan Watts

For we are His poem.
                    —Ephesians 2:10

From Part One:
Flying Mountains, the Stability of Mist

A Birthday Poem for Amelia, 1983

> *Cherish the little one holding your hand....*
> *This is the lot of mankind.*
> —*Gilgamesh*, Tablet X, col. ii

Holding hands,
we walk the April puddles.

"Look at the mountains
flying!" It takes

a two-year-old to see
stability in mist, and other

evaporating life.
I take my yarn hat

and dry the playground swing
after Juneau rain.

Riding Stable
Teresa's Sixth Birthday Party
Douglas, Alaska, July 7, 1985

Giving horsie rides, I join
the children's stable: fathers, uncles,
relatives, and friends, the first
time in years I've horsed around
like this. I see myself a saddle-
bred, five-gaited, racking
out, and now a Tennessee
Walker, under mountain ash
and clothesline. I want to strut
my stuff, but Dominic wants gallop,
so we canter with a left lead
in a blending of our fantasies
of horse shows and the open range in
this class for two-year-olds and up.

Anchorage Dump, Limited

Salvaged especially for the Gutenberg Dumpsters:
Ron, Suzie, Rachel, and Tommy; on the most illustrious
occasion of the visit of the Two Garys—Snyder and
Holthaus—to the Gutenberg Dump, Haines, Alaska, April 29, 1984

Only go to the dump when you can leave
nothing of yourself, but long since
regenerated cells—the fingernails,
discarded hairs of memory. In homestead

days each piece a treasure—like this dead
appliance just the thing to shore up undercut
embankments on the home-made bridge, or fill
a bottomless pit in the soupy break-up road.

Though all these things are useless in the city—
survival for another time and place—
I look at pickups all around and ask

how can everybody else just toss
away such things I still evaluate
so highly on my scale of blazo box?

Dragging Anchor

After nights
of sleeping on the boat,
we're home again
and sleeping on the water bed.

Rolling to the window,
I wake in terror
from my rocking sleep
to see the Sitka spruce.

Class Reunion, June 21, 1985

—for Kathie

Like yearbook pictures, poems of the past
leap out. "Where did the horse and rider go?"
Your pony's memory, like melted snow,
the rider here and now, and now outclassed

only by your own maturity
and lighter touch, your eighth grade gym floor box
step now dressage. We talk, with midnight lox
and bagels, highlights of a quarter century

in one midsummer night. I came the longest way.
The youngest, with the oldest child, is you.
Though neither father, lover, still I do

feel from then that certain rights accrue,
but my reunion trivia's not true.
We both live equidistant from today.

Villanelle on Lines by Wendell Berry
(from "Letter" and "Rising")

> *One puts down the first line of the pattern in trust*
> *that life and language are abundant enough to complete it.*
> —Wendell Berry, "Poetry and Marriage"

The lives I will not know in satisfaction
but only in desire's clarity,
the fields whose past and potency are one,

are graveyards, cornfields in Marcellus, Latin
hamlets in the hills and maple trees.
The lives I will not know in satisfaction

are roots of living trees of immigration.
For each of us, there was a first to leave
some fields whose past and potency were one.

For each of us, some forebear had to question
which life to live, and which would be
a life he would not know in satisfaction,

which potency a past then in creation,
as hunting, working forests, farms, or sea
so fields whose past and potency are one:

no potency at home, the destination
without a past, the fear that both will be
lives I will not know in satisfaction,
no fields where past and potency are one.

From Part Two:
The Fruits of Winter

Birth of the Theotokos

You shall be a crown of beauty
in the hand of the Lord
and a royal diadem
in the hand of your God.
                    —Isaiah 62:3

Long after we thought
the yard would bear
no more, we discover
yet another crop
of snow peas. We pick them
in late September rain,
drops collecting in the metal pan.

I contemplate: a harvest
of raindrops in the north!
If we could just preserve them
in this desert of ice.

But these are pearls
to crown a feast of stir-fry,
a diadem
celebrating birth.

Mind Weeds

September: gray and rainy
Sunday afternoon, the Feast
of the Birth of the Mother of God;
on television Jerry Falwell
predicts precise dates
and participants of Armageddon.
In the rain,
yard work: transplanting
evergreens, expanding
strawberry beds. Through the rain,
aromas: dinners cooking—
the neighbors' and our own. The sauna
warming up for later; but for now
muddy fingertips
and a seedling, salvaged
from the compost pile.

Middle Child

Katrina: forever
in the middle of things, midway
from Carpathians, the Kuskokwim, and midway
in potato rows. Shining
like stars in dark-earth skies,
the fruits unearthed, held
joyfully in hand: the finite
earth, of infinite
return. The center of creation, ever-
moving, roots
in central moments in earth-dark
shining eyes. Absolutes
turn relative. Katrina,
forever central, soon
no longer
middle, with the turn
of time and season, and the ripening
of seed: the smile, ephemeral,
eternal, in eternal return.

The Visit

—for Gus and Margritt

The widowed mother rakes
Alaska leaves. I think of Ransom's
"Antique Harvesters," the season
of declension on the land.
She rakes. We gather inward.
Slowly, we accept
the falling of the leaves
and learn to handle
the fall of human life
like trees, emptied
of obsolescent images
of spring. We gather inward
into gray October
Sunday afternoons, tightening
our circle, till the focus
falls upon the single leaf.

Two Covenants

1
In two covenants, the turning
of the year, atonement over;
and beginning of the new.

2
The Leave-
Taking of the Cross:
I carry leaves
to mulch the berry beds.
Winter surprised us
coming over the Starnbergersee,
et cetera, the leaves
heavy with falling snow.
Caught, as if between
two covenants,
I stack the woodpile
in the piling snow.

3
A coda: the unexpected smells
of summer: caked grass scraped
from the power mower bottom,
the smell of oil and gas;
the mower stored, the spark plug
ready for another year,
bikes and garden hose
hung for winter, preparing
the beat-up shovel for the car
trunk, lamenting only
the tune-up isn't done.
In the carport, garbage cans
rattle in the wind.

4
Nearing dark, when suddenly,
Brueghel-like, a black
bird startles, flies
across the snowfield
into brush-stroke trees
of winter.

5
This is a day
of atonement,
at–one–ment
with the world:
living out eternal
images of winter, and impending
death. Nightfall,
and the day begins; autumn,
and the year is new.
The promise: everything
is only put away.

The Liturgy of Snow

Snowflakes are like ghosts
trying to put together
a puzzle of themselves.
—Genesis Ransom, age 6

1
Become aware
of intervening spaces
and the space around us
as they come alive
with falling snow.

2
The paradoxes: endless
falling, constant
variation—the seeming
stillness of eternity.
If you've seen one
snowflake,
you've seen them all.

3
The single
snowflake-trace
moving through our vision—
an actor
against absorbent black.

4
Within this range
of spruce and barren birch,
the eye absorbs
the snowflake, dis–
membered and remembered
by perspective. In the sky
it can't be severed
from creating sources;
on the earth
each single snowflake
piles its
almost weightlessness
as if
tensioning a spring.

5
Falling snow: shifting
dimensions of itself
perceived as what we know
and therefore never known;
the snow
falling from itself
settles
in itself,
will rise again
invisibly upborne
into itself
as emptiness.

6
In falling snow
we try to understand
this birth
without beginning.

Snow becomes
experience itself,
a form of emptiness
against which
houses and the trees
are constructs,
measurements
we posit for our seeing
suspended in the midst of
particles of time;

the positive
of reading constellations:
starlight, shining in the void,
discrete,
arranged as symbols
articulating emptiness.

We see as process
what we once considered object:
personality, and space.

7
What is this appeal
of falling snow?
More than beauty,
this perception
of the single snowflake,
this perception
of the field
of falling snow;
like snow itself
seeing it
settles through the mind
and irrigates the brain
for burst and flourish, breaking
through the sleep of time
into eternal present
like a rose,
the empty one
receptive
to the silent voice
saying, "This is You"
face to face
in the infinity
of falling snow.

Driving in a Snowstorm,
King Salmon to Naknek

—for Gary Holthaus

We leave the things of earth
behind: the river bottom, alder,
willow, birch, and evergreen

for white becoming white,
the road defined by weeds
like runway lights,

brown against the snow
on either side; the car
hurtles like a float plane

on a lake of snow, a taxi
on the step of tires, rushing
almost weightless, to the point

where the white strip curls
upward: lift off, where the road
parts from snowbound earth.

Night Flight, Fort Yukon–Fairbanks

—for Dick Mueller

Night flight,
Fort Yukon–Fairbanks;
to port, Orion
and the half-moon;
to starboard
northern lights;
the symmetry of dials
and moonbeams
reflected on the wing.
Below us, frozen lakes,
snow-defined and countless,
thicker than the stars:
the Yukon Flats—
a Milky Way of snow
settles through the black
infinity of spruce.

Skating with My Granddaughter Genny on the Feast of St. Michael the Archangel, Anchorage, 1981

In falling snow,
we practice figures
on a skating rink,

in floodlights work for grace
before an audience of night
with every snowflake a shining

cherubic face
or angel wing
punctuating darkness.

The rink becomes a diskos,
and every settled snowflake
a piece of some communion

bread, each morsel bearing names
of every person living
or who ever lived.

In Memory of Our Godchild Jessica on the Feast of St. Michael the Archangel and All the Bodiless Powers of Heaven, Anchorage, November 21, 1982

In retrospect,
a dream before your death:

we were all out skiing.
You were skiing, too, your snowsuit

frosted, angel–like, angelic, out
before us, but still just within

the forest edge, on a rising
turn, just about to start

the long and gentle glide
into the clearing, brilliant

with a million suns
exploding on the frosted snow.

Meditation on Our Godchild Jessica

(April 22, 1976–December 29, 1982)

Jessica, a bride of
Christ, incapable of
sin, in thought, word, or
deed. And yet, is this
perfection? A living
doll, angel-like and brain
damaged, your entire
life a gift of love. A question,
a thought to which my mind
returns in prayer of you,
thankful for the gift of
the ability to sin.

Sunrise, Chugach Mountains, December 22

He who wraps the heaven in clouds
is struck upon His back.
          —Matins, Elevation of the Cross

He who wraps the heavens in clouds
is wrapped in the purple of mockery.
          —Matins, Holy Friday

We near the timeless moment toward
which all of our chronology
declines, and out of which our
measurement increases. Birth is near
of Him without beginning. Black and blue
the back of heaven, streaked with red;
the sun, like lava, like some
orogeny where clouds themselves
arch cloud mountains from
an earth of mountains. Red seeps through
like some prefigured blood welling
from the passion of the world-tree
whipping-post axle of the world,
the timeless pivot point of time,
and slowly floods the present dawn
with fullest reds of glory, drains
to white, and empties
from the shortest winter morning
into darkness of the longest winter night,
to be remembered in the golden chalice
of our longest summer day.

Triptych on the Nativity Icon

1
Like Joseph
in the corner of this icon,
I want to understand.
Being human,
I am overwhelmed.

2
The image of Joseph
in ever-moving
experience:
the artifice is ordered
to tell us all things change.

3
It is revealed:
"to whoever overcomes
I will give the morning star."
As if
the cattle understand
with only Joseph
still bewildered.

Forefeast of Theophany

—for Bishop Gregory and all political prisoners

*Tufts of wadding sprang into sight in the back of his jacket, marking
the path of invisible bullets. . . . While the bullets came lower and lower . . .
we lay with our faces buried in the snow . . . that Epiphany morning.*
—Solzhenitsyn, *Gulag Archipelago Three*

*Come, naked children of Adam, let us clothe ourselves in
unapproachable light that we may warm ourselves.*
—Romanos, Theophany Matins

Bethel, Alaska,
forty below;
blizzard, and the chill
factor ninety-five
below zero
Fahrenheit
and falling.

Bethel, Beth-el,
House of God.
The face prays
a litany of pain.
Each human body
becomes
a living icon
encased with silver rizas
of its own breath,
exposing only face.

Our images
    are antiphons
to other times
    and places;
from Bethel
    to Byzantium,
the eyes of flesh
    see water;
the eyes of faith
    behold the spirit.
The Jordan sees Him naked,
    who cannot be seen.

As if in summer, God
is very near—so close in fact,
we lose the structured count
of Sundays after Pentecost;
but now the north
is low angle in the sun–
centered universe, and water
flows in darkness
under ice; above it
dog teams move
northbound through the tundra
to Kwethluk and beyond
where water is prepared
as we remember
the Theophany of Christ,
the River Jordan, on the Kuskokwim
at ninety-five below.

Playground

The sliding hill
in January sunlight:
volcano-like, alive
with lava streams
of brightly flowing
children.

Of Being Born in April

—*for Levi Morrow Hensel*

The final weeks of pregnancy,
lovers and the earth
alone together,
read the signs of coming
birth: break-up
of the river-ice, exploding
willows, and the tiny
footsteps from within.

I think of Voznesensky:
from Askhabad to Bethel,
bellies swelling in the full
moon. But here
is love: abandon
only to the joys
of solitude together—the solar
energies of March,
the final days of oneness
before the earth is filled
will all creation, and the lungs of life
scream to take it in,
and the boundaries of love
are redefined.

On Lazarus Saturday

Wading through the knee-
deep snow, I gather
Palm Sunday willows.
The payroll moose already
occupies the grove,
slowly stripping trees;
slowly chews, *ful*
savourly, slowly turns
and looks. The bark dangles
from its mouth.
O taste and see!

Keeping Watch
(Holy Saturday, 1983)

Keeping watch: the eagles
pivoting in radar sweeps;

on rocks, the cormorants
like blips, and the herring fleet

bobs at anchor, hopes
rising and falling

with the tides. The only
herring spawn is fog:

filters down the mountains,
gathers on branches,

settles to the bottom.
Clouds become

the gentlest of rains
on Sitka streets, the people

scurrying like shellfish,
scavenging the floor.

Russian Easter 1981
(St. Innocent of Irkutsk Orthodox Church,
Anchorage, Alaska)

As if
these northern lights confirm
what the music tells us
circling the church
with the myrrh-bearing women
on our three-day journey
to the empty tomb:
> *The angels in heaven*
> *sing Thy resurrection,*
but we on earth
still await the news
beneath the physics
of solar flares and shock waves,
energy showers
sprinkling the earth—
> the earth still frozen,
> crunchy, where we meet it,
> thawing underfoot
> after equinox, after
> Passover, but still
> not fully released
> from the hold of death—
while songs and incense rise;
as if perhaps
from some angelic vista,
this stream of candle flame
becomes some
human northern lights
rising from the earth,
a flowing glimmer in the vernal
almost-midnight dark.

Archetypes of Ephemera

I take the same
pictures every year:

grass thrusting
among the hollow stalks,

red berries
by weathered logs in sunlight,

fireweed in bloom
and sunlit amanita,

summer trees
in shade and sunlight,

translucent leaves
against the blinding glare.

I take the same
pictures every year

in some response
to the matter of our lives.

Father Michael Oleksa
Blessing the North Pacific

1

Imagine this, as Rie
Muñoz might paint it:
black cassock, green
stole flapping in the ocean
breeze, Elijah's ravens
doing somersaults, a flock
of fishermen. Father
Michael blesses the North
Pacific Ocean; happy
Rie Muñoz waves
rolling on the beach,
and maybe a bear or two
watching from the woods.
(A little dogma here: the world's
already holy; we're just
enjoying it.)

2

Some data
from Oleksa, Epistle to Spenard:
"Last summer
when fishing was going badly,
we went,
on the Feast of St. Elias
(accompanied
by several beautiful ravens),
to the beach
and blessed the Pacific.
The total
salmon catch for the season

broke all records,
and no one here
considers that coincidence.
Last year
one boat refused
to be in the annual
blessing of the fleet.
It sank
before the season opened.
You've got to take the White Folks
into consideration.
There might be something
to all this stuff."

3
Creation, as re-
organized by artists, priests,
and poets, in some enormous
misty Buddhist scroll,
people burning incense
in the lower corner:
Old Harbor, Alaska,
Center of the World.

At Kenai Lake

—for Ralph and Ramona

A dawn so silent
only the sound of raindrops
shaken from a birch behind me
radios the unseen
lighting
of the Steller's jay.

Move carefully among the spruce,
each needle with its tiny
ornament of rain, each drop
a globe comprising earth.
A galaxy of raindrops
in a firmament of spruce.

Camping at Wonder Lake, Denali Park on the Feast of John the Baptist, 1982

With silver blades, frost
and snow sever the life
of summer feasting: tundra
red this Day of John

the Baptist. Like sap, flowing
from extremities, swans and Sandhill
cranes pulled in skyway
veins follow the watershed

of earth. The aftermath: adjustments
to change in being: bears
browsing in the last of berries,
fattening for sleep and resurrection;

trinities of color: golden
birches, aspen, willow
haloing the reds of lichen,
blueberries, and the stunted birch;

snow-filled passes, and the lower
earth veiled in chilling
mists and drizzle (to vanish with the next
frozen sunrise, when the leaves

clatter to the ground like castanets
while the last wisps of clouds
swirl from Mount Denali—
The Great One in glory). But now

blades of ice shatter
at the touch of body heat
as with cold fingers, campers
roll their soggy tents.

through the screen doors
in central New York
where it's always summer

of childhood memory,
the land that people enter
when they die.

The Archeology of Childhood
(Syracuse, New York, July 1972)

A time for the evening under the lamplight
(The evening with the photograph album).
—T. S. Eliot, "East Coker V"

1
At thirty,
a man hung up on death
and children,
neither his own.

2
I study photographs:
my parents at thirty
and theirs at twenty-five.
I realize
I am old.

3
A photograph:
my grandmother,
her sisters,
all dead now;
a fleeting glare of sunlight
on the corner of a lens:
hazy brilliance and the shade
of central New York
broadleaf summer trees:
the four sisters
sitting on the lawn
with sparkling eyes.
Fulton, New York,
circa 1910:
sunlight as nostalgia.

4

Again the birds of childhood
sing in the summer trees,
the eastern songbirds
of years ago, and still
the sounds of children playing.

I have returned
from timberline Alaska
to older time zones;
I have climbed the stairs
to this summer
bedroom in the trees.
But now I go
willingly to sleep.

Divine Liturgy at St. Elias Orthodox Church, Onondaga Hill, New York, Blind Man Sunday, 1982

Where faces change
on people and the earth
we enter

into cosmic time
and celebrate this banquet
where as kids we played

softball at family picnics
in pastures with bases
of dried up cow manure.

Now St. Elias rides his flaming chariot
where Uncle Johnny
used to drive his tractor.

Beyond the altar, an enormous
stained glass icon window
of Jesus, Cleopas, and Luke

going on before us
in place
of what has gone before.

In the end,
we move to other lives,
and in the present,

returning to ourselves,
we try to see
through a window of divinity

what lies beyond—
because we think we know
what used to be Uncle Johnny's barn.

Lunch at Aunt Peg's, 1982

(Candee Street, Phoenix, New York)

—in memory of Peg Grier Dight (June 13, 1900–February 16, 1985)

1
In August sunlight, sounds
of summer locusts
like an air-raid siren.

I sit and contemplate
sixty years of pictures
on a Phoenix porch

and photographs from Fulton
of relatives long dead
by a family house long sold.

2
I contemplate
timelessness and time.
The house itself

a giant sundial,
a fixed center—stability
over which the sun

measures out a portion
of eternity by lifetimes
passing through its rooms,

or sitting in its gardens,
avoiding shade
of maples, English

walnut, bathing
like a clock face
on a summer afternoon.

3
Inside, the house as ever:
cool, inviting, and the clock
ticking out the minutes;

antique mirrors, emptied
of so many faces the photographs
retain much longer; the antique

table, that has offered up
so many meals
and where again the relatively

permanent sustains
the necessary
transient.

4
In cemeteries: Phoenix, Fulton,
sunlight nearing Trans-
figuration, over shaded graves.

Night Watches

*You are . . . the epistle of Christ . . . written not with ink, but with
the spirit of the living God; not in tables of stone, but in fleshy
tables of the heart.*
    —2 Corinthians 3:2-3

*Always bearing about in the body the dying of the Lord . . . that
the life also of Jesus might be made manifest in our body.*
    —2 Corinthians 4:10

Ye are partakers of the sufferings so shall you also be of the consolation.
    —2 Corinthians 1:7

1
What can we add
to the well-worn
images of death?

Nothing
but our own experience

and hopefully
images of death
worn well.

2
Six bells. I meditate
in the watches of the night.

Around the hour, chiming
rooms of heirloom clocks, clocks
of other times and places, some
on eastern standard, some
on daylight saving, clocks
from this house and that
from this aunt and that
all wound and ticking,
measuring our lives, and chiming
watches of the night.

On the nightstand,
the alarm clock set
for medication.

3

The room is papered now
with memories.
The pattern of this room
is children taking comfort
in the early years,
and returning it
in final days.

In this room, your mother
was invalid before you.
In this room, you nursed her
while your children watched
in this room
where Grandma prayed the hours,
and by the hour
we listened to the radio;
Lone Ranger evenings
and cold winter mornings
dressing for school,
we hurried to the warmth
of this room
while you prepared
the Mother's Oats.
Then television. Now
we monitor these tubes
and measure morphine.

4
The nightstand Kleenex box: designs
of women athletes. Beside them
your skeletal remains.
You lie, your face contorted
in pain and terror, wrapped
in drainage tubes, life
draining from the body
that gave us birth.

The flesh becomes
a cosmic throw-away,
the physical a shell, the outside
of the box, the pretty picture
that's the first to go,
leaving only spirit
that leaves the body too
at the fullness of time
in the pregnancy of death.

5
The pain quickens,
the labor pains of birth
into life beyond.

Your children
measure out injections,
turn your body,
searching for what flesh remains,
to stab it quickly.

6

The dark night of the body
is alive with images.
A thunderstorm: lightning jabs
oppressive August heat
like a gleaming needle in the dark
and humid body of the night.

7

Six AM Our father
keeping watch: his morning
washing of your face. The cooling
washcloth passes.
You smile,
look up to him,
and die.

One Could Think

*My Grace is sufficient for you, for my power
is made perfect in infirmity.*
—2 Corinthians 12:9

One could think
of more romantic ways
to die
than cancer of the colon.
But this reminds us
how each of us is born
with the image of Divinity
inter feces et urinam
and that the soul
is not the only organ
to magnify the Lord.

A Dream on Your Birthday, February 15, 1983

—in memory of Jane Dauenhauer
(February 15, 1918–August 11, 1982)

I tried to reach you
    every way I knew:

by telephone, by phone,
    with CB

patch, computer mail,
    by micro-

modem over satellite,
    but you

were camping in the Adirondacks, out
       of reach.

Howard Dight in Memoriam
(1903–1979; died gardening, June 1979)

Gardening ... is the voice of the Buddha.
—Robert Aitken

1
The sun moves
toward vespers
toward the Sunday
of the Paralytic Man,
to resurrection hymns
in Tone Four,
and as the earth itself
turns through time and space
I turn the soil,
prepare the garden bed,
make it ready
for receiving seed.

2
In the north, planting
on Memorial weekend,
for the first time I feel
how this is so erotic:
the little mounds, cleft,
receiving seed,
this living out
eternal images.

3
Consider: we are victims
of our language. Through words
like "soiled" and "dirty,"
we forget our roots.
Each lifetime
is totally our own
yet totally a gift.
Human: humus:
humid: humility:
keep the living ground
humid, so the seeds
can germinate.
We are all seed
and custodians of seed
from somewhere else.

4
Gardens in summer sunlight:
muggy, hazy
afternoons, the sun
beating on the gardens
in central New York State—
in Phoenix, in Syracuse,
in Onondaga Hill—
drawing them to fullness
through July to August.

5
Again, the seeds,
the letting go of life
to gain it,
life itself
as dying generation.
We turn
our faces to the brilliance
as much as we can bear.
Forever first fruits,
we glitter
in Divine Transfiguration.
We make our requiem
thanksgiving for a life,
and of our dirge
alleluia.

Afterword

The poems gathered here span fifty years of published writing, over forty of them lived in Alaska. The poems are like a surveyor's benchmark; each is some kind of intersection of time and space, each marks a certain place in time, a certain time in space. Many are nonconceptual, even diary-like; others are very meditative and highly conceptual.

This isn't the place to discuss literary influences, but some highlights are important. In college, certainly Frost and e. e. cummings were important. I was a student of Philip Booth, who was a student of Frost. I like Booth's rhythms very much. Browsing in one of the college neighborhood bookstores the summer I graduated, I discovered Gary Snyder's *Myths & Texts* and I have been in love with it ever since. In the late sixties, I grew increasingly interested in perception of the object as a theme in poetry, especially in William Carlos Williams and Wallace Stevens. The mantras of this discourse include "no ideas but in things," and "the thing in itself, not ideas about the thing." In style, this plays out in metaphors and similes and in debates about whether poetry is seeing one thing in terms of itself or in terms of something else. In Europe, I especially like Rilke and his poems about seeing things and Boris Pasternak, who studied with the neo-Kantians at Marburg. I think this influenced his style from his early poems to the very end, living and writing in Stalinist Russia. On the whole, he hasn't been well translated.

I am not dogmatic, but I have enjoyed exploring different points of view, depending on what the situation seemed to suggest. At one point in the early seventies, I think, when I was frustrated with the philosophical discourse, I remember the following short poem coming to me, but I can't locate it among my drafts. From memory:

> Poem, composed
> while putting on my shoes:
> There is a muse,
> goddammit
> and it's not Immanuel Kant.

A more recent suggestion that appeals to me is by the Orthodox Abbess Mother Raphaela (Wilkinson): "Let us seek soundness for our eyes (Mt 6:2) so that we may see creation, others, and the world around us as windows through which the glory of God shines" (*Becoming Icons of Christ,* 55).

In addition to my interest with phenomenology in modern poetry, two other themes that run through my life and poetry are language in the abstract and the various languages that I have studied and translated, and that remain a central part of my life, especially German, Russian, Finnish, Swedish, and Classical Greek. I have been interested in oral literature most of my adult life, and since coming to Alaska I have worked extensively with Tlingit oral literature, co-editing several volumes with my wife, Nora Marks Dauenhauer. We have been partners in marriage and scholarship for almost forty years. I have also worked with central Asian oral epics. Some of my poems are about poetry, and some are about translation.

I decided to open this collection with new poems rather than to proceed chronologically. The new poems date mostly from the mideighties to the present, and most were first published in a variety of little magazines and literary journals. The "New Poems" of this collection gathers all of my poems published in journals or local editions but not yet published in book form. I have also expanded this section with some previously unpublished poems. Many of my poems written in the seventies and eighties and published in book form appeared in *Phenologies, Glacier Bay Concerto,* and *Frames of Reference,* which make up the "Selected Poems" section. The new poems gathered here were mostly published before and after those collections. In all cases, I selected the poems I like the best and that friends and readers most frequently request. They are arranged in a compromise of theme and chronology.

The "New Poems" half is arranged in five sections. Part 1 celebrates family and friends and is loosely biographical; part 2 is comprised of images of Juneau, Nora's home and where we have lived since 1983. Part 3 is about my father's death; part 4 is selections from a cycle in progress about the death by cancer of a close friend, Ron Scollon. Part 5 is about gardening, especially the harvest. One of my hobbies is growing heritage potatoes and keeping alive the seed of a Tlingit potato brought from Chile and California by the Russians, possibly with the help of the French explorer La Pérouse. When Elizabeth Kunibe, one of our students at the University of Alaska Southeast, did DNA testing as part of a national potato genome project and discovered that we were growing a hitherto unknown species of indigenous potato, we got to name the variety "Maria" in honor of the departed friend who gave us the seed that had been in her family gardens for over one hundred years, Maria (Ackerman) Miller.

Especially for parts 1, 2, and 5, in the words of Theodore Roethke, the physical context of many of the poems is "I live between the heron and the wren" on Douglas Island, opposite downtown Juneau, in a beach habitat we share with deer, land otters, and black bears. The poems in part 3 were composed in upstate New York on a woodlot next to the spot where Grandma Moses painted her "View of Cambridge Valley."

The "Selected" section of this book opens with early poems published in little magazines from 1963 to 1969. For a number of reasons, I decided to put the early poems published in little magazines 1963–1969 in the "Selected" section rather than the "New," even though they, too, with a couple of exceptions, have not appeared in book form. This section includes a few unpublished early poems that I still like after fifty years and would like to see remembered as benchmarks of those times and places, even though I would not or could not have written them today. I also took the liberty of relocating some poems published in *Frames of Reference* to this section because they date from this period or they fit better thematically. These are poems of the "wandering years" of college and graduate school (New York, Finland, Texas, Finland, Wisconsin, Alaska) and there is no real thematic cohesion in the section. For historical reasons, I was tempted to begin with this section, but it seemed more exciting to begin where I am and not where I have been.

Looking back, I see the war in Vietnam as the defining, or watershed, event for my generation. At some point or other, most of us eventually had some personal experience that positioned us somewhere in the confusing range of domestic reactions to the war. I was in the audience in Berlin when JFK made his famous "Ich bin ein Berliner" speech. I was between classes at Syracuse University when I heard the news of his assassination. I was in the audience at Syracuse University when LBJ made his Gulf of Tonkin speech. In my first month in Madison, the police and national guard tear-gassed the campus and began clubbing students as they vacated classrooms and buildings. In retrospect, the war seems like a demonic tar baby—so easy to get into, escalated by deception, so hard to get out of, and impossible to get out of with clean hands.

About *Phenologies*
The poems in *Phenologies* were written in the early seventies during a two-year residence at timberline on a mountainside overlooking Anchorage. I lived without electricity or running water, near the end of a seasonably impassable road. These poems unabashedly fall in what Kenneth Rexroth once called the "Gary Snyder Bear Shit on the Trail School of Poetry." The poems explore an aesthetic based on observation without comment or evaluation, and without metaphorical distortion: They are an attempt to see things as they are rather than in terms of something else.

As a collection, *Phenologies* occupies an important position in my poetry of Alaska. It is a prelude to the long poem format of *Glacier Bay Concerto* and a companion to the more conceptual poems of *Frames of Reference* that move in a more transcendent direction, examining the relationship between the natural and liturgical years.

Phenologies has a very interesting publication history. Of my three books of poetry, it was the first written and the last released. I place it first here because most of the poems were written before those in *Glacier Bay Concerto* and *Frames of Reference*. Its publication history is the stuff of the exciting world of little magazine and small press publishing. My friend Paul Foreman, of Thorp Springs Press in Austin, Texas, who had published many of my translations in his magazine and anthology, liked it and wanted to publish it. Then the printer kept the press run as hostage until Paul could pay the printing bill. The book languished until Paul's "ship came in" in the form of inheriting a very promising series of platinum claims and therefore the cash or credit enough to pay the printer and market *Phenologies*. Copies are still available. Paul Foreman died of cancer on December 21, 2012, as this book was in the copyediting stage.

About *Glacier Bay Concerto*
After concentrating on *Phenologies* to hone and clean up my style, I wanted to go in the opposite direction and try a long poem dealing with Alaska historical, political, and spiritual themes. But I was also ethically concerned with

the problem of writing about other people's mythologies without understanding one's own, so *Glacier Bay Concerto* was as much a learning experience about Judeo-Christian tradition as Tlingit, drawing me deeper into both. It was a one-way trip into scripture: Tlingit and Judeo-Christian literature—oral and written—where I remain today. It was also deeply personal, because I had been adopted into the Chookaneidí clan, whose traditional homeland is Glacier Bay. I was given three Tlingit names, two of which come from Glacier Bay and Lituya Bay: Xwaayeenák, my father-in-law's relative who was drowned at Lituya Bay, and Kateedí, which alludes to the image of waves lapping over the edges of a small iceberg floating in sunlight.

I was delighted at the mixed reviews of *Glacier Bay Concerto*. People either loved it or hated it; one reviewer denounced it as the worst poetry he had ever read; one kayaker wrote me that he had it held open under bungee cords so he could read along as he paddled Glacier Bay. I guess that's my favorite piece of fan mail. Some other reviews are very flattering, and I feel a little embarrassed at the generous praise, but I'd be a fool to disagree. "A combination of history, social commentary, and visionary poetry infused with an ancient voice which...refuses to die....A heartbreaking tour de force....His vision is unrelenting." "A work of magnificent scholarship and magnificent feeling....The product of a deeply religious mind...that sees in the microcosm of Tlingit history the reflection of the entire...history of America....Runs the gamut from screams of outrage to tender songs of love...a wonderfully unified book, a poignant cry for justice, a love poem any woman would weep to receive." "There is discreet sublimity here, singular, insistently unique. Fresh...and...impressive. One looks forward to his new poems."

In 2009 Nora and I were honored to have Rick Trostel, of the Juneau Student Symphony and the Alaska Youth Choir, commission Australian composer Thomas Reiner to set some of our poetry to music. From my work, he selected a passage from *Glacier Bay Concerto* (some of which I stole from Psalm 121) "I will lift my eyes to the mountains where my help is from." The choir sings this regularly as their closing piece. Several years earlier, the late Pastor Louis Born, at that time a Presbyterian minister in Klawock, sent me a cassette of him singing parts of *Glacier Bay Concerto* to music that he composed. He captured what I had in mind very nicely in his music. *Glacier Bay Concerto* is long out of print, although copies show up in used bookstores from time to time. As this book goes to press, Thomas Reiner has set another of my poems to music, "Dust" (p. 101), to be performed at a festival in Greece.

The Shroud of Shaawat Séek' first appeared as a chapbook of that name, hand printed and sewn in a limited edition during a printing workshop at Orca Press, Sitka, 1983. The original edition was subsumed and expanded as part 3 of *Frames of Reference* (1987). In the present collection I have added the "Hoonah Graves" poem, which fits the theme and is roughly from the same time period.

About *Frames of Reference*

The poems in *Frames of Reference* explore different ways of seeing and experiencing, imagining and remembering. The poems measure time and place, focusing on complex intersections of the natural and liturgical years; calendar and clock time; human lifetime; history and memory; dreamtime; photography and text. Through images of plants and animals, people and the land and of the unique energies of children, the aging, the dying, and the dead, the poems frame the ephemeral and the permanent, transience and roots, in physical and spiritual reality, and celebrate life that is always here and now.

The book version of *Frames of Reference* includes a prelude and five parts. For the present collection, I have relocated a few poems from part 5 of the book and organized it here in three parts. As excerpted here, part 1 is about family and friends, part 2 follows the natural year and the liturgical year, which in the conservative Judeo-Christian traditions begins in the fall; and part 4 deals with death and dying of family, especially my mother. As noted above, *The Shroud of Shaawat Séek'* was reprinted as part 3 of *Frames of Reference* and here is restored to a section of its own. Although the small press publisher (Black Current Press, founded by Ron and Suzanne Scollon) is no longer in business, some copies of *Frames of Reference* are still available.

To the extent that they are rooted in experience and place, there is always a risk of unintentional obscurity or of personal references that may not be shared with all readers. Sometimes the most personal images can be the most universally accessible, and the seemingly more universal, the least accessible. For example, the image of some relative that no reader has ever met until that poem may turn out to be more accessible than a more universal liturgical term a thousand years old and still in use, but perhaps not familiar to the reader. I considered including notes or a glossary, but readers have assured me that even some terms not found in standard dictionaries are now readily accessible through the electronic wonders of Google.

It has been difficult to select from over fifty years of writing, but the struggle has mostly been the sweet experience of what Robinson Jeffers called "the honey of peace in old poems." Although I have usually thought of these words as describing poetry from sources such as the *Greek Anthology* or indigenous oral literature, I guess I'm old enough now to apply the description to some of my own. Welcome to *Benchmarks*, some poems from the middle of the journey of my life.

About the Author

Richard Dauenhauer, born (1942) and raised in Syracuse, New York, has lived in Alaska since 1969. In 1980 he was named Humanist of the Year by the Alaska Humanities Forum. From 1981 to 1988, he served as the sixth Poet Laureate of Alaska, succeeding Sheila Nickerson and John Haines in that position. He is among the poets laureate featured in the April/May 1985 issue of *Coda*. In 1989 he received an Alaska State Governor's Award for the Arts. In 1991 and 2008 he was a winner of an American Book Award from the Before Columbus Foundation. He is widely recognized as a translator, and several hundred of his translations of poetry from German, Russian, Classical Greek, Swedish, Finnish, and other languages have appeared in a range of journals and little magazines since 1963. He holds degrees in Slavic Languages, German, and Comparative Literature. Since coming to Alaska, much of his professional work has focused on applied folklore and linguistics in the study, materials development, and teacher training of and for Alaska Native languages and oral literature. He has taught at Alaska Methodist University and Alaska Pacific University in Anchorage, and part time at the University of Alaska Southeast in Juneau. From August 1983 to March 1997, he was Director of Language and Cultural Studies at Sealaska Heritage Foundation in Juneau. In 2003, he rejoined Sealaska Heritage Institute as a linguist. In August 2005, he accepted the position as President's Professor of Alaska Native Languages and Culture at the University of Alaska Southeast, from which he retired in 2011. He is married to Nora Marks Dauenhauer, a widely published and anthologized Native American writer and transcriber and translator of Tlingit oral literature, who was named 2012–2014 Alaska State Writer Laureate. With Nora, he is co-author of several volumes of instructional materials for the Tlingit language and co-editor of the multivolume, facing translations series, *Classics of Tlingit Oral Literature*. He lives in Juneau and works as a freelance writer and consultant in addition to his occasional teaching.

Book Publications in Creative Writing

1988   *Phenologies.* (Poetry) Austin, TX: Thorp Springs Press.

1987   *Frames of Reference.* (Poetry) Haines, AK: The Black Current Press.

1983   *The Shroud of Shaawat Seek'. (*Poetry chapbook, typeset, printed, and sewn by hand) Sitka, AK: Orca Press.

1980   *Glacier Bay Concerto. (*Poetry) Anchorage: Alaska Pacific University Press.

1978   *Snow in May: An Anthology of Finnish Writing, 1945–1972.* Edited by Richard Dauenhauer and Philip Binham. Cranbury, NJ: Associated University Presses.

1976   *Hyperion: A Poetry Journal, Translation Special* 4, no. 13. Edited by Paul Foreman. Austin, TX: Thorp Springs Press. (At time of publication located in Berkeley.) I was a major contributor to this special issue, with forty-nine translations from various languages. A book of my translations is noted in the Introduction as a forthcoming project of the publisher, but it never materialized, due to the financial ambiguities of small press publishing.

Major Book Publications on Tlingit by Nora Marks Dauenhauer and Richard Dauenhauer

2008   *Anóoshi Lingít Aaní Ká, Russians in Tlingit America: The Battles of Sitka, 1802 and 1804.* Edited by Nora Marks Dauenhauer, Richard Dauenhauer, and Lydia T. Black. Seattle: University of Washington Press. (Winner of the 2008 American Book Award.)

2006   *Sneaky Sounds. A Non-Threatening Introduction to Tlingit Sounds and Spelling.* Richard Dauenhauer and Nora Marks Dauenhauer. Juneau: Sealaska Heritage Institute.

2002   *Lingít X'éinax̱ Sá! Say It in Tlingit: A Tlingit Phrase Book.* Edited by Richard Dauenhauer and Nora Marks Dauenhauer. Juneau: Sealaska Heritage Institute.

2000   *Beginning Tlingit.* 4th Edition, with CDs. Nora Marks Dauenhauer and Richard Dauenhauer. Juneau: Sealaska Heritage Foundation Press.

1999   *Alaska Native Writers, Storytellers and Orators: The Expanded Edition.* Special Issue of *Alaska Quarterly Review.* Edited by Jeane Breinig and Patricia H. Partnow. An expanded version of the 1986 edition edited by Nora Dauenhauer, Richard Dauenhauer, and Gary Holthaus. Anchorage: University of Alaska-Anchorage.

1999   *Tlingit Spelling Book.* 4th ed. (1st ed., 1974; 2nd ed., 1976; 3rd ed., 1984). Nora Marks Dauenhauer and Richard Dauenhauer. Juneau: Sealaska Heritage Foundation.

1994   *Haa K̲usteeyí, Our Culture: Tlingit Life Stories.* Edited by Nora Marks Dauenhauer and Richard Dauenhauer. Seattle: University of Washington Press.

1991   *Beginning Tlingit.* 3rd ed., with audio cassette tapes. Nora Marks Dauenhauer and Richard Dauenhauer. Juneau: Sealaska Heritage Foundation Press.

1990   *Haa Tuwunáagu Yís, for Healing our Spirit: Tlingit Oratory.* Edited by Nora Marks Dauenhauer and Richard Dauenhauer. Seattle: University of Washington Press. (Winner of 1991 American Book Award.)

1987   *Haa Shuká, Our Ancestors: Tlingit Oral Narratives.* Edited by Nora Marks Dauenhauer and Richard Dauenhauer. Seattle: University of Washington Press.